T0369352

Sometimes
Love Lands
Sideways

Sometimes Love Lands Sideways

*Josy & Greg
Drove Off Into
The Sunrise*

Kevin Bailey

SOMETIMES LOVE LANDS SIDEWAYS
JOSY & GREG DROVE OFF INTO THE SUNRISE

iUniverse books may be ordered through booksellers or by contacting:

iUniverse
1663 Liberty Drive
Bloomington, IN 47403
www.iuniverse.com
844-349-9409

ISBN: 978-1-6632-6215-8 (sc)
ISBN: 978-1-6632-6216-5 (e)

Library of Congress Control Number: 2024908085

Print information available on the last page.

iUniverse rev. date: 04/18/2024

Contents

Introduction

My first book was named, *Josephine Daudry*. This book is the next part of that story. Now, at the end of that book, I left Josy and Greg, the two main characters, driving off into the sunrise. I had not planned on writing a sequel, but as folks read the story of Josy, and wanted to know what happened next…I decided to give it a go.

If you have read that first book, or if you haven't, it would be good to read or re-read the first book so you can understand the references in this second book that refer back to *Josephine Daudry*.

I thank my granddaughter Sophia for the title of this book. It was an offhanded remark about her finger skateboard which she named 'Love' because it had a picture of two dinosaurs kissing on it. She would hit one end with her finger to flip it, and it would land on its wheels, and she said, "Love always lands." Then, one time it landed on its side and she said, "Well, sometimes, Love lands sideways." I immediately picked up on that statement and asked if I could use it. She said, "Sure Papas."

I think the title so appropriate for many relationships and marriages that come about unexpectedly. While this is a work of fiction, it is drawn on many real life happenings.

Like my first book, I thank my wife and family; as well as the many friends who have encouraged me to write this next chapter of Josy's story. In fact, I am planning the final part of this series of three books, even as I write this introduction.

I hope you enjoy them all!

Kevin Bailey   April, 2024

Chapter 1

George Abernathy and Charles Goodwin

George Abernathy looked up from the photo of Ellie, Laney, and himself. He was wiping the tear away from his cheek when his nephew, Charles, walked in.

"You...were...right...Charles."

"What was I right about, Uncle George? And hello to you too!"

Charles was taken back a little. It had been a while since his uncle had said much of anything to him, or anyone for that matter. Many thought he could not talk at all.

Certainly, being in the nursing home with only his memories for company most days drew George inward again. But now, Charles could tell something had changed. His uncle was talking again...a bit slowly...but clearly.

"She came...Charles, she came to...see me, and...after all... these years."

"Who came to see you?"

"Josy...you know...Josephine...Daudry."

Charles smiled. "O really...I thought she might, someday."

George was struggling a little to speak. Charles put his hand on his uncle's shoulder and said, "Take your time Uncle George... take your time."

"I'm fine. I was...going to say...well, I was not expecting it." Then he mumbled to himself. Charles thought what he heard him mumble was, *"My Josy."*

"Well, I'm not surprised. After all she comes from...well... anyway. She is a good kid. I used to see her in Humphrey's when she worked there. She turned out all right. Even after all that transpired in...uh... '74..."

George interrupted, "Yeah...'74...I've tried...to forget...all that."

"Oh, I'm sorry Uncle George. I didn't mean to drag up bad memories."

Charles was a bit afraid his comment might trigger his uncle back into silence. But instead, George went on.

"Yeah, well, no matter...anyway, you...just missed her. She left...only a few ...minutes...ago."

"Really? So, what did she say?" Charles asked with a sigh of relief.

"Well, she asked me...to forgive...you know, her dad...and all. And she said...she forgave me. Forgave me...Charles...she forgave me! She only...found out about...the accident and...our Laney...just recently."

"I still don't understand why Aunt Ellie made you all promise to be silent for so long, because in the end it came out in a way none of you wanted."

"I know. What can...I say? I am not...proud of...who I... became...after the...accident and...especially after...your aunt... died."

"How did Josy find out?"

"She said...Sarah...finally told her...after Harry died...last year."

"Wow, that must have been a shock to her. They never told her...and after all this time. And you say she forgave you.

"And...she...asked...me to...forgive...Harry too."

"Wow."

George looked at the family photo again, and remembered the day that photo of Ellie, Laney and himself was taken. It was her 6th birthday party only a few months before her death. The whole family was there. They all had such a great time.

George turned to Charles and said, "You...took this...picture."

"Yes, I did. That was a great party. I gave Laney so many horsey-back rides that day; she wore me out."

They both got quiet and just looked at the photo for a while. Then Charles sat down next to his uncle and asked, "And, so... Uncle George, did you...forgive Mr. Daudry...have you been able to?"

George looked out the window and after a long pause he responded, "I guess...I have...yes, I do." And after...all...the things...bad things...I did...back then, it's...me...who needs...to be forgiven. And she says...she did. But I...I...don't know...about Sarah."

"Oh, I am sure that Mrs. Daudry has, she understood your pain. My mom told me that she wrote Aunt Ellie after the accident. From what she shared with my mom, I can be fairly certain she was...if not forgiving, at least understanding."

"I hope...you're right. I certainly...gave her reason...to hate me. And she sure... got mad at me back then...but...I just...couldn't let go of...you know."

"Yes, and she was just being protective of her daughter, you can understand that. And you did get better." Charles got up and began to wheel his uncle out of the room.

"You know, Uncle George, I think this has been a good morning."

George put up his hand for Charles to stop. Then he looked

back at his nephew and reached for his hand. "Yes, it has. And you know...I feel...at peace. For the first time...in a long...time I feel...completely at peace. And...it is you I have to...thank for getting...me to...a place where I...am today. I mean, you... Anita...and especially the twins. Just being...a part of...their lives...that is, what I say...saved...my life."

"I'm happy for you Uncle, very happy. And you know the twins just love you to pieces. You are more than a great uncle to them, That's why they call you Uncle Gramps."

George smiled and said, "Oh I...love them...so much, I feel... like a Grampa...to them. They say...time heals, but...for me...it was...Rachel...and Robby."

Now Charles was tearing up, but said with a laugh, "Okay. I will send you their bill for therapy!" But, really...thanks for saying that Uncle George. That means so much to me and Anita. Both the twins wish they could be here more often, but you know they're both so busy in college."

They were heading down the hall to get lunch in the nursing home's cafeteria when George asked, "Can...we go...to lunch at the diner...today?" Charles stopped and turned the wheelchair toward the nurses station. "Let's find out" he said.

Humphries diner was very busy that day in February. The parking lot was so full that Charles had to park on the street. The wind was cutting right through George and Charles as they made their way down the sidewalk to the door.

"I'm...ready for a hot...cup of coffee" George said.

"Me too" Charles agreed.

When they finally got seated, George began to talk. "So, Charles, you…know I have not…talked a lot…for a while since… my stroke. But…with Josy's…visit today, I am ready to talk… about you making…all my…final arrangements. I don't…know… how much longer…I have…and I want to…make sure the trust… is all set…for you…and the kids…and also…you know…the other one…."

Charles interrupted, "Yes, Uncle George, I have it all ready at my office. Everything you have set aside for your will and trusts are ready upon…your…."

"My death" George finished Charles sentence.

Just then, Frank came out from the grill. "Hey George! It's good to see you out and about. How are you? You're looking good for an old guy."

George chuckled and gave Frank a nod. "Thanks Frankie, it's good…to be out, and you…look good too…for a…middle aged guy…with a beer belly."

Frankie laughed. "Hey, that's no beer belly…it's my patented burger belly."

George laughed back and said, "Well, I can see that…and… your burgers…are great. So make it…just…like I remember."

"Oh I will, I remember how you like it!" Frank responded.

Charles looked at his uncle and commented, "He's a funny guy, that Frankie, he's always so happy…even when he must be pulling his hair out on a busy day like this."

"Yes, he has always…been that way." George said as he waved at Frank.

As they ate their lunch and looked out the window at the cold winter day, Charles thought back to the day when he got the call from George that aunt Ellie had died. She was the glue that held the family together.

Charles' mother, Audrey and Uncle George were not always close. They were close at home, when George was young. Audrey was older than George, and they really grew apart when she married Al Goodwin. George and Al did not get along. Al teased him a lot, but it was the fact that he was taking his older sister away that really got to George. Then, as he grew older, he at least tolerated Al. And when Charles was born that gave the relationship between them a new bond. And then, when George married Ellie, the family ties grew tighter.

Ellie, was such a peace-maker, and got along with everyone. And even though, the childhood tensions were eased between Al and George, it still was a cool relationship. They were on opposite sides of just about any topic, except Charles. They all doted on the little man. As time and life proceeded, George did not make much effort to stay in touch with Audrey and Al. But Ellie, made sure on holidays, that either the Abernathy's or the Goodwin's would make the effort to be together as a family. And over the years they began going camping together and spending more time as a family. They played a lot of games and the old tensions didn't seem to matter as much as the fun they had being together.

When Charles was a teenager, Laney came along, which drew them all closer. Charles liked being a big cousin to Laney. When the accident happened and Laney died, they all became very close. Except for George. He had retreated into himself and was not the same uncle that Charles had known. Charles was 21 years old when Laney died and though the two families still got together on holidays, it wasn't easy with George being so reclusive.

Charles didn't understand. "Why is Uncle George still so mad?" he asked his mom one day, and Aunt Ellie seems so...I don't know, like she always is."

"People handle things differently I guess, Audrey replied. Ellie has a grace that not many have. It is a gift. Your uncle adored Laney and just can't understand why she was taken. Audrey looked out the window, took a deep breath and said, "I don't know what I would do if I suddenly lost you. I just don't know."

Charles was 32 when he married Anita Baker. Charles' mom, Audrey, had been admitted to a nursing home with early on-set dementia. She was able to be at the wedding but was not completely present. It was the last time she and Al were together. Al died, in 1970 right after Charles and Anita married.

Life, overall, was happy for the young Goodwin's. The newness of their marriage helped Charles during his time of grief that year. But when the call came in, that Ellie had died, everything changed. The years of grief or lack of grieving took its tole on Uncle George, and now, without Ellie, things got dark. Charles was his only nephew and took on the responsibility of trying to care for George.

Between visiting his mom in the nursing home and a heavy work load along with being newly-weds, Charles and Anita did what they could, but with George being so reclusive, it wasn't easy. Then, after the incident in '74 and the arrest, it became a necessity to help his uncle. He represented George at court, and helped arrange counseling after the 'drive-by' incident. Sarah and the Sheriff insisted that something be done considering George's behavior. For a few years George seemed to do well. He went to Alcoholics Anonymous and counseling until 1976 when he fell off the wagon...hard.

George was at Humphries' Diner that summer of '76 on a Monday morning. He sat at the counter as usual. He looked over the specials on the chalk board and then gave his order to Mama H.

"Hey Eleanor, have Frankie cook me up my usual, will you?"

"Sure thing, George."

He sat there drinking his coffee and tickling his eggs with his fork, when he suddenly was taken aback. He saw a familiar figure through the grill window. It was Josy Daudry putting on an apron. She had just started working there for the summer. She didn't see him. But he saw her...standing there, putting her long brown hair up in a pony tail. Then there were her brown eyes and her slightly upturned nose. All he could see was Laney. But it wasn't his Laney. Seeing Josy there in the diner, starting her young and promising life, just sent George into a tail-spin of rage.

All he could think was, *It could have been, should have been my Laney with all the possibilities of life ahead. But no...it's Josy... her life has been deemed by God or whoever to be more important!* But then he thought, *Josy...oh Josy.*

George just could not get it out of his mind. Tears began streaming down his cheeks. He stopped eating and got up and left, almost running out the door.

Mama H., came by his stool and said to Frank, "Hey, where did Mr. Abernathy go?"

"Hmm...I don't know. Maybe to the men's room?" Frank replied.

Mama H. held his check figuring he'd be back to pay later. But George never came back...for many years.

As Charles continued to eat his lunch he looked at his uncle and remembered how George frequented the bars late at night and drank heavily from '76 into the year of 1979. Nothing Charles or Anita said, kept their uncle out of the bars. And the more George talked about the accident and Harry's mistake, the more folks listened. Some of the people were around back in '59 and remembered Laney's death. They wondered back then what happened. Now finding out the truth of it all made them a bit angry too. Others just felt so bad for George that they took on his grief and sense of the unfairness of it all. It made George feel good to know they were on his side, as it were.

Everything came to a head in 1977 when Harry tried to talk to George. Just seeing Harry there sent George into a rage, and the folks in the bar basically escorted Harry out. No one wanted to hear his side of the story, even though Harry was trying to be apologetic in his approach. It all backfired on Harry and the people turned against him, especially business wise. There were no great outward campaigns to bring the garage to ruin, but the lack of business did just that.

In '78 Harry and Sarah gave up and sold the garage. After paying off their loans and mortgage, there wasn't much left. It was a bad time for them financially, and that seemed just fine to George. He stopped going to Humphries' so he didn't have to see Josy. He would drive by the old gas station and gloat at what he had been able to do...a measure of justice, in his mind. It went on like that for the next year…until his great niece and nephew, Rachel and Robby turned 6.

George wasn't great with babies and toddlers, but when the twins turned 6, they reminded him of Laney. Before the accident, she was this precocious and funny 6 year old who he would have long, crazy, fun-filled conversations and playtimes with.

George always used to say, "Ellie, this girl will be on the *Jack Parr Show* someday. She's got a natural talent."

Ellie would look at her little girl and say, "Yes, my Laney will be anything she wants to be."

They adored her to no end. And that year, George got to know his daughter like he never had before, that is until her death. Now, the twins, at 6, were just like Laney. And that fact did not make George sad or mad. Instead it gave him a deep down joy that had been lost to him for such a long time; and that new found joy also got him to go back to Alcoholics Anonymous.

As the twins grew and George spent more time at Charles and Anita's place, the time came for an announcement. They sat Uncle George down and talked to him about moving in with them. He was getting on in years and all the stairs at his old house were getting harder to navigate.

"Our house is all on one level, and we have plenty of room and we would love to have you Uncle George. So would the twins."

Rachel, as she gave George a hug, said, "Please come live with us, Uncle Gramps."

"Yes, we all want you to live here," said Robby.

Anita also agreed and assured George that it would be no trouble.

George was hesitant at giving up his house and all the memories there, but he did love to be here with his family...the only one he had.

Getting the old house emptied and sold was a lot of work. It took many months, but finally the day came to move in. Robby had made a big banner out of rolled paper he got from his mother's teaching supplies and it read, 'WELCOME HOME UNCLE GRAMPS!' with all kinds of sunflowers painted around it. That was Rachel's contribution. She loved sunflowers.

As George got settled in over the next few weeks all seemed to go well. Having their Uncle right there with them, took a lot off of Charles and Anita's plate and stress levels. They were always worried that Uncle George would fall or worse in the house and they would not know about it. Having him at their house was so much better.

When George's house sold, Charles remembered asking him, "How do you want me to handle the proceeds, Uncle? I can put the money in the trust you had me set up for your investments."

"No, George replied, I've been thinking a lot about that old station, you know, Harry and Sarah's old place. I'm thinking...it's been empty for a while...and...it may sound crazy...but I think...I want to buy it...and then..."

"More coffee?" Said the waitress as she came by with the carafe. Charles was jolted out of his memories.

Chapter 2

A Balloon and a Ring?

"Okay folks, you two hold the end here as high as you can. Here comes the heat from the salamander. It will begin to fill the balloon and then, when it fills up enough, you can let go and I will fire up the burner to fill it the rest of the way."

Josy and Greg followed Richard Handley's command. He was the pilot of the balloon and had been flying for more than 20 years. That fact made Josy and Greg a bit more comfortable as this would be their first ever balloon ride. They had driven very early that morning south to the Finger Lakes to take in the sunrise over Seneca and Cayuga Lakes from the air. Later that day, they also would take time to visit a vineyard in the region. It was a beautiful Saturday morning; the stars still out and the moon was full as they drove south. They arrived at the balloon's launch site at 6:00 am. It was a crisp fall morning. Coffee was waiting for them, which they greatly appreciated.

The balloon was laid out flat on the ground on top of a huge tarp. The ground crew had just finished unfolding it. Josy and Greg lifted each corner of the balloon's opening as high as they could. It was heavy but they held it up and it began taking form as the heat poured in. After about 5 minutes with the gondola still on its side, and the opening fully formed, Josy and Greg let go and the pilot lit the burner. The flames shot into the balloon's opening with force and heat. And little by little, the balloon started standing upright until the gondola also was righted. They were ready to go.

The boarding steps were pulled up to the 'basket,' which is what the crew called the gondola. Richard said, "Climb on into the basket from the steps, and please be careful." It was a tight fit but Josy and Greg got in and settled themselves. Then, Richard checked with the ground crew, and pulled on the burner controller which lifted the balloon up about 6 feet as the ground crew held on to the ropes. When it was stable and everyone was ready, the ropes were let go. Richard gave a burst of flames into the balloon and the ground dropped away.

"Wow, this gets in the air quick!" Greg said as they ascended past the tree tops. Josy just looked around at the colors of fall. The sun was just beginning its arc over the horizon. "There it is!" Josy exclaimed as they looked to the East.

Richard pushed the play button on his small boom box and The Fifth Dimension started singing *Up, Up and Away.* Josy joined in on the chorus. Then Richard and Greg joined in too. They had a good laugh after the song ended.

"Nice touch, said Greg. I haven't sung that song in a long time."

"This is just amazing!" Josy said as they climbed higher. "How high will we get?"

"Oh, about 2500 feet or so. We'll be above the low clouds."

"Which way will the wind take us?" Greg asked.

"We'll find out." Richard replied. "The forecast is for winds out of the West but there are currents at different altitudes that can go contra to the prevailing wind. We are on an adventure. I am not exactly sure where we'll end up."

Josy and Greg looked at each other. They were both thinking

the same thing. *This balloon ride is kinda like our relationship, taking us wherever it leads.* Greg reached out for Josy's hand and she gave him a good squeeze. They smiled and looked to the sunrise. It reminded Josy of the ride in the newly restored Pinto a year and a half ago after her birthday party.

They had driven back up to the lake the morning after St. Patrick's Day, taking the Pinto wagon through its paces. Not at 100mph, like she did when the deputy pulled them over, but close to 85 a few times. Many roads in Western New York are flat and straight. Perfect for going way too fast. They got to the lake about 11:30, walked on the beach, and then got lunch at the same restaurant Josy had slept all night at in the parking lot on the night she learned about Laney Abernathy's death. It became their 'Place,' with their favorite table on the inside and another favorite table on the patio outside. Depending on the weather, they would sit at one table or the other. They had met there many times over the many months of planning the Pinto's restoration and talking about business. Since that first drive in the Pinto, they also took time to come to their 'Place' just to get to know each other and it was clear they both wanted a long and lasting relationship.

One time, while having dinner, Josy brought up the subject of children.

"I have to ask you Greg, we have been together, really, since my birthday. And I think, well I know, I like you...a lot...I mean, a whole lot."

"My feelings for you are the same."

"Well, okay. Then I need to know something before we talk about, well, marriage. But even more importantly, to me, is what you think about children. I mean, you know, we are not that young, and I'm not sure what I want. There is a lot I would like to accomplish before thinking about marriage or a family. I mean, the detailing business and helping my Mom is paramount for me. Greg, I'd really like to know what you think."

Greg sat there for a moment smiling at Josy. "Well, to be honest, I have thought about marriage...but as far as children, and I can't believe I have not told you this yet...it's kinda my secret, I have never told anyone outside of my mom and dad. I'm not sure why..."

Josy looked suspect at Greg and then around the room. She did not like the sound of this.

Greg continued. "Okay, here it goes. I have children. Two to be exact." He let the shock sweep over Josy's face and then laughed and said, "One is a girl in Haiti and the other a boy in Ethiopia. I have been sponsoring them for 5 years now."

"You big...booger! You really had me scared there." Josy exclaimed as she gave him the 'look.'

"Sorry...I couldn't help myself. You set yourself up for that one."

"Why didn't you tell me?"

"Oh, I don't know. We were always so busy with everything. I have always kept my letters to and from them to myself. I kept it secret initially because it was just after my sister died. I don't know, I just didn't want my folks to think I was trying to replace my relationship with my sister."

"Were you?"

Greg sat back and stared at the ceiling. "I...maybe...I don't know. Annie was such a wonderful sister. She looked after me like a mom. She always encouraged me and would always give me little things she made. You know, mementos. She would say, 'Someday you can look at this and remember you can do anything you put your mind to.' You know, she would give me little things like that, sometimes on my birthday and sometime for no reason at all. I kept them all. Anyway, I was reading some magazine... one day, and I saw this picture of a man leaning down to give his sandals to a girl who had none. It was in some resort town in India or somewhere like that. He was well dressed and she was literally in rags. She was in tears. It was not a huge gift for him, obviously he could easily buy another pair of sandals, but for her it was a big deal, And...well...that photo tugged at my heart. And then I saw these pictures of little children in poverty. It was an ad for helping them. Something just came over me and I just started crying, convulsively. I had never done that before. I think it was grief but also, compassion. I couldn't help my sister much in her last months. She was in a bad way. She just drifted away from us. It was so frustrating. I felt helpless. When I saw the pictures, I just knew I had to help these children. And I could help; it was like giving a pair of sandals away for me. It was only a dollar or so a day but for these children it could be a big thing. Any way I called and talked for a long time with the representative. I told her that I wanted to sponsor a girl and a boy, I didn't care from where. I said, 'Just pick them for me.' I wouldn't have been able to decide."

"Wow, that is so... Josy kinda teared up. That is so good of you to do."

"Well, I have to say, beginning that journey with these two kids, gave me a way through the loss of Annie. And I think my sponsorship also gave me, I don't know, courage or whatever to venture out on my own in business. My life really changed back then."

"I guess so. So tell me about these kids of yours, this little girl and boy." Josy smiled as she said it. It gave her a deep joy to know this man, would do something so generous.

"So, they were young when I started. Elisma was 3 when I began to sponsor her. She is now 8. She lives in Haiti in a poor neighborhood of Port Au Prince. Well, most every where is poor in Haiti. The boy is Bekele and he lives in Ethiopia. He is now 11. He is already working, subsistence farming. He lives where AIDS is rampant and of course there are the child exploiters out there. Militias...Traffickers...so many factions. These are very dangerous places to try to grow up and have a childhood of any kind. At least with my monthly support they get to have a community safe from all the poverty and bad influences that are all around them. They also get medical care, education, meals, spiritual teachings, and maybe, a way to a better life, even in their countries."

"You sound like an advertisement."

"I'm sorry. I guess...well, I am passionate about it."

"That's okay. I am proud of you. And I have to admit, I have seen some of the programs on TV but never responded. I feel bad for the kids...but...I don't know. I guess I am not as compassionate as you."

"Well, I doubt that....and I think if it wasn't for my sister... maybe I would have never...the loss of her made me more open...I guess"

They both went deep into thought for a few moments. Then Josy came back to her question... "So you never did answer me about us having children."

"I am with you Josy. It's late for us both, but of course, mainly for you. I am content with helping kids like Elisma and Bekele. I am open to adoption as well, if you decide to think about that."

"Good. That takes a load off my mind."

They finished their meal without saying much more. Then they left the restaurant hand in hand. Greg noticed Josy held his hand more tightly that usual. After a long walk, they turned to each other and kissed. It was more passionate than the little pecks they had with each other before. This was going somewhere special, they both could feel it.

As Josy and Greg stared at the view out of the gondola, they were just awed by the sunrise and the land before them. The colors and contours were a beautiful painting. They were taking pictures and noticing landmarks and especially the lakes.

"How fast are we moving?" Josy asked.

"Oh, I'd guess we're going about 25 miles per hour." Richard said.

"Where do you think we will end up?" Greg asked.

"Well, this trip lasts about an hour and at the pace we're going, we should land somewhere on the East side of Cayuga Lake. The wind is blowing us north eastward, so we may end up somewhere near Auburn. That would be good. 'cause there is a good place to get our breakfast on Route 20 near there."

When they passed over the East bank of Cayuga Lake, Greg said, "I guess it's time."

"Time for what?" Josy asked.

Greg got down on one knee...sort of...in the gondola there really was only room for a weird curtsy. Josy just looked at him...

shocked and excited at the same time. Greg had pulled a tiny velvet box out of his pocket. He held it up.

"Here? Really? In a balloon?" Josy asked.

"Ah...well, I guess...maybe not." Greg tossed the box over the side.

Josy shook her head in shock...gasped and gave Greg a dirty look. He just stood up with a big grin plastered all over his face. Josy was very confused, as she saw him doing something with his hands. He was winding up the fishing line he had attached to the box earlier. As he did, it became clear what he had done.

"You, You....YOU!!!" Josy exclaimed.

"Josy, will you marry me?" He asked as he fully retrieved the box and opened it to reveal a ring.

"NO!:" You son of a...urrgh...you...you!...Come here."

They kissed and kissed...tears of joy flowing from their eyes. Greg had his answer.

Richard, was in on the prank. He laughed and congratulated them both. "That was a first." He said. "I was not happy about throwing a ring overboard, but I saw how your fiancé actually stitched the line in, wrapped it around the hinge, taped it on to the bottom...I guess you could say, he did not plan on losing it."

As Josy pulled the ring out and Greg put it on her finger, he said, "By the way, this is a temporary ring...just in case. The real one is back at home." That was a bit of a fib.

"Oh yeah, it does look a little..." Josy eyed the ring... "well, a lot...fake."

"Yeah, I got it out of a gum-ball machine."

At that, Josy gave him a little scoff up side the head. "The real ring better be a really great one, let me tell you Greg Watkins!"

"I can tell you it did cost a bit more than a quarter." Another little fib.

"Ah...You! You are such a kidder. You are a pain in my butt! But I love you."

"I love you too." Greg said as they kissed again.

Richard spoke up, "All right. It's time to begin our descent. I will bring us down slowly as I look for a good flat and open place to land. Here is where it can get tricky because the wind currents near the ground can get a little unpredictable."

As they descended, Richard reminded them of how to land. "Now when we get close I will tell you to prepare for landing. As I said in the pre-flight, lean away from the side of the basket that will hit the ground first. It will be a jolt, so brace yourselves. If we have to land on a hill, it can be harder to control what the basket does. So be ready for any kind of sudden movement. The main thing is to hold on tight."

They skimmed over tree tops and roads just above the telephone poles. Then there was an open field that had just been harvested. "That looks good." Richard said. But as they were about 30 feet from the ground the wind pushed them away toward a tree line. Richard quickly pulled on the burner control to lift them above the trees and out of trouble. They continued looking for other landing spots. A school football field looked good for a moment, but the wind had other plans for them.

Finally, they came across a farm house with a large back yard. It was on a slight incline but Richard didn't think it would be trouble. So they came down. This time the wind cooperated and they touched down.

The jolt was strong and Josy bent over the side as if she was falling out. Greg lunged to grab her and pulled her back up.

"Are you okay?!!" Greg and Richard exclaimed at the same time.

Josy just laughed. "I had you there, didn't I? And you deserved it…both of you."

Richard was not amused. "That is not something to kid about. Even a few feet off the ground, you can get hurt. My crew will be here shortly, so please just stay in the basket." Richard got on his walkie-talkie to let the crew know where to park.

Josy and Greg just held each other, while snickering silently.

When the ground crew arrived, Richard gave a short burst to lift the balloon and the crew grabbed the ropes and pulled them over to a flat open spot. Then they all got out of the gondola. Josy and Greg helped lay out the big tarp and Richard began deflating the balloon. It was a busy few moments, and folding the balloon up and rolling it up to fit in the trailer was hard work. But they finished, and then Richard gave the home owners a bottle of wine and some other gifts for being the 'Hosts' for our landing. They were gracious and talked with everyone for a bit.

"Please forgive me." Josy said to Richard.

"Of course, but…"

"Yes, I will never do that again."

"Good! All right…let's get breakfast."

They had a nice visit with the whole crew at the diner on Route 20, and Richard asked about how they met.

Josy answered, "Well, just like our landing today…our relationship kinda came at us sideways."

"Yep, some tough news and a dead battery brought us together." Greg said.

"Well, now you have us interested." Said Richard.

Josy looked around at the table and said, "Okay, so it is a long story, but I can give you a shortened version. Here goes…My father had died, *she had to pause as everyone gave condolences,* and I had received some disturbing news and drove up to the lake on a whim. I stayed all night in this parking lot of a restaurant and in the morning my battery was dead because I left the radio on all night. So I needed a jump…and who came to my rescue but Greg."

Greg butted in, "Yes, and we had not seen each other since high school."

"Anyway, one thing led to another, and here we are." Josy said.

"So, is that your hot rod back there, Greg?" Richard asked.

"Oh no…it's Josy's"

Josy gave Richard the 'look' and said, "Why did you assume it was his? That drives me crazy."

Richard was taken back…but then he apologized. "I am so sorry. That was wrong of me. I am sorry."

"Good! 'Cause that happens to me all the time."

"You are talking to a real mechanic. Greg said. Josy and I rebuilt that car from the ground up. We overhauled the engine over many a late night together."

"Is that how you fell in love?" The waitress asked…she had been listening in as she refilled the coffees.

Greg answered, "Kinda. We knew we liked each other since high school. We took an automotive course together at BOCES and always had fun working together."

"But he was too scared to ask me out." Josy said.

"Yes…I was very shy and insecure. But after I helped Josy that day…"

"I called him. Josy interrupted, he was still too shy."

"Yes, I was. Still am...but not with you anymore." Greg leaned his head on Josy's shoulder.

"When did you know...you were...you know...in love?" The waitress asked.

Josy and Greg looked at each other and sighed simultaneously. They said it in unison. "Maybe someday we will tell you." Everyone looked confused. Josy said, "It's an inside joke." Then everyone chuckled and they finished their breakfast with more small talk. Then they drove back to the launch site. Everyone was quiet, just taking in the scenery and the morning air. After handshakes and goodbyes, Josy and Greg drove to a vineyard for a relaxing rest of their day. Reminiscing over wine and lunch, Josy and Greg talked about the past year, and the day they really knew they were in love.

They remembered it was last summer. After Josy learned of Greg's 'children' she wanted to be involved. So she sponsored a little girl herself. Milagro, who was from Nicaragua. She and Greg would compare letters they had written and received along with the pictures. Josy only had a few since she just began her sponsorship. And because there was civil unrest and fighting in Milagro's country, it was uncertain if the program could continue. Josy was very scared.

Josy said, "I know what it's like to be really scared. Maybe not like civil war...but still really scared."

Greg asked, "What happened to you?"

"Well, it's a long story, but you know the bad news I have said led me up to the restaurant that night? I guess it's time to tell you." And she did.

After Greg listened to the whole story, he just gave Josy a hug. "You have been through a lot."

"I don't know about that. You have had your share of troubles too."

"I guess we both have had our share, haven't we? But I believe going through tough times can make us better. Sometimes, bitter...but hopefully better...not bitter better but better better."

Josy chuckled, "You always find a little humor in just about anything. I love you for that."

Greg smiled at Josy, "I love you too."

They both just said it so naturally without thinking. That's when they knew.

On the ride home from the ballooning and wine tastings, Josy said that she wanted to start really working harder at the detailing shop and form an exit plan from the DMV. "I want to start putting more hours in. I have a line up of jobs waiting and I need to really focus on them." She said.

"No worries, The folks know this is a start up. And these cars are not their primary vehicles so, you have time."

"I need to get going. I really need to."

"Okay, so what is your plan?"

"I am giving my 2 week notice on Monday. And then I am going to use up all my personal time, vacation time and holiday time to give me a good 2 months of pay. That way I can get some of these jobs done and have a payday waiting for me when that money is gone." And I have my retirement funds for the future.

"Sounds like a plan. Monday?...Okay...I will get things ready for you over the next two weeks." Greg eyed the toy ring on Josy's finger. "So, umm…do you want to set a date right away or wait?"

"Let's get the real ring first, shall we?"

"Yes, of course…I will bring it over to your mom's tomorrow for our Sunday dinner."

"She is going to be so thrilled. She just loves you Greg. You know that, don't you?"

"Well, if the apple pies are any indication…I do know that. And I love her too. She is a great person."

"Your, mom and dad are great too. Maybe we could invite them over to Mom's and you can get down on your knees…all the way this time…make it official."

"Fine by me."

As they parked in Josy's driveway, Greg picked up Josy's hand and kissed it.

"May I get the door for you, Madame?"

"Oh my goodness! Don't push it buddy" Josy got out and shut the car door briskly. Greg just snickered. He was getting to know all her buttons and loved pushing them…in a fun way. He would never really disrespect her though, he loved her too much for that.

Now, he had to get a real ring. He thought about the bushing he had polished up at home. Which was the ring he referred to on the balloon ride. It was a ring, but not a real one. He was going to offer it to Josy for fun, but after the balloon ride and seeing her reaction to the fake ring, he thought better of that. Instead he thought of a better plan. As they hugged and kissed good bye, Josy supposed Greg was headed back up to the Lake.

"See you soon" She said

"Okay, bye."

At that, he was off…to the jewelry store.

Chapter 3

A Mechanic's Wedding Plan?

Sunday came and Sarah had a feast prepared. Greg showed up with his parents, Theresa and Roger. Mama H. was also invited. Everyone had a great dinner talking and laughing. Except Theresa, she was subdued. Even though she had been getting counseling for years now, she was still a bit uncomfortable in social situations and was not...as they say, 'the life of the party.'

Months before, Greg had brought Josy to meet his parents after their talk about children. Roger was a proud Welshman and Theresa was a mix of Tonawanda Seneca and French or English...she wasn't sure. Josy had noticed Theresa's complexion and distinctive facial features; as well as some craft hangings on the wall which she assumed was possibly from the Tonawanda tribe, since they had a reservation nearby. She asked Greg about this.

"Your mom is a Native American...isn't she?"

"Yes, she is from the Tonawanda Senecas, the Hawk Clan, I think. But she also has some French or English blood mixed in there."

"That's funny, my ancestry is French and English too...but no Indian blood."

"Well, Mom doesn't say she's Indian, because she's not from India"

Josy laughed a little. "Yes, I see. That makes sense. So, to say, 'Native American' is correct?"

"Mom doesn't like that either...she says, 'We are people of the land.' She had a very hard life...someday I will tell you what I know. It's not much, because she doesn't talk about it. But I think whatever it is, it may be part of the reason for her life long battle with depression."

Josy was a bit timid around Theresa after that. She didn't know how to talk, or what to say. But she did get along fine with Roger who was just a big bear of a man and was very fun loving. She could see where Greg got his sense of humor from.

After the dinner at Sarah's home, Greg gathered everyone into the living room and made Josy sit at her window seat. Then he got down on one knee and pulled out the ring. A real one this time. Now, as subdued as Theresa was, when she saw her son ask Josy to marry him, her face lit up and she was teary eyed. She jumped up from her seat and made a yodel like holler. Everyone was a-gasped at first, but then, seeing her pure joy, they all got up and danced and cheered. Sarah put on some Celtic music and they continued to dance away.

"Now that was some proposal! Mama H. exclaimed. Is this what your reception is going to be like? Wow, Theresa, you sure can belt it out. How did you learn to do that call?"

Theresa, seeing she was being looked at by everyone, suddenly shrunk back and sat down. Looking at the floor she said quietly,

"My grandmother taught me that. It's an old call...she used to call all the children in for supper with it."

"I would like to hear about her sometime." Mama H. responded.

Roger sat down next to his wife and put his arm around her; looked at her eye to eye with a reassuring smile. Josy, feeling a little uncomfortable with the sudden quiet, started showing off her ring to everyone. They were all saying how beautiful it was and then Josy said, "Well, this is the second ring, right Greg?"

"Yep. I got her a fake one the first time around."

Everyone just had a blank stare.

Josy explained, "So, this is actually the second time Greg proposed. The first time was on our balloon ride...and the ring he brought was out of a gum ball machine! And he threw it over the side!" They all laughed at that. She then related to the folks the whole story.

Roger asked, "How did you know Josy would react that way, so you could toss the ring?"

"I didn't. I was planning on faking a trip and losing it over the side. But then, Josy's reaction made it perfect. You can't plan those things. Just have to go with the flow, and...I know Josy's buttons, so..."

Josy gave him 'the look' and said, "You better watch it there, buddy."

They laughed some more and then Sarah said, "It's time for dessert." They all went back to the kitchen.

After dessert, they all sat in the living room with Greg and Josy on the window seat. Greg pulled out a folded paper from his pocket and said, "So, I have been thinking about our wedding. Here are some vows I want to run by you all."

"Don't you think we should discuss this alone?" Josy asked.

"Nah...it's okay...you'll see. Here goes, these are my 'Mechanics' vows:

When your battery is dead
    I will recharge it for you
When you have a loose bolt
    I will take my wrench to you
When you're all clean and shiny
    I will drive you down a long dirt road
When your bearings are shot
    Will I trade you in?...NOT!!
When your gaskets are starting to leak...
    Well, that depends...*Depends*...get it?"

Everyone just stared at Greg for a moment. Then his dad broke out in laughter, and then they all joined in while shaking their heads in disbelief.

Greg continued, "I was thinking of having the wedding at a drag strip, and our wedding bands could be bushings...we could race our cars down the 1/4 mile and screech to a halt, get out and do our vows. What else could we ask for? Right?"

"You are still joking, aren't you? Josy asked. What an imagination you have! You are crazy...certifiable."

"I got a condition...I'm nuts and bolts for you!"

They all left Josy and Greg sitting there and went into the kitchen. Sarah commented to Mama H. that Greg was something else with those plans. Roger said, a little under his breath, "I thought it was a good plan." Theresa just smiled and skipped along behind them all, but as they turned to see her she stopped and looked at the floor.

"You are not serious about a drag strip are you?" Josy asked.

"Well, I guess not."

"You were serious."

"Well, It would be different. It would be fun. Right?"

Josy sighed and looked out the window, the lights from inside hid the details but she did notice the orange and red leaves falling from the tree branches. A dog was running across the lawn. She hadn't really thought about a ceremony yet. During her growing up years she only fantasized about marriage but never really took it seriously. What did she want? She wasn't sure. But a wedding at a drag strip was definitely off the table.

Greg sat there, not knowing what to say next. He touched Josy's hand and just gave it a light squeeze. She pulled away and stood up.

"I am going home. I need to think."

"Are you mad at me?"

"Well, a bit. You should not have said all that before we talked. Even if you were joking...do you think our wedding is a joke? Something to laugh about?"

"Whoa! I...of course not."

"Listen, I just need some time."

"Okay, I am sorry. I can drive you to your apartment."

"No, I will walk. I need some fresh air. I will see you tomorrow."

Greg got up and walked her to the door. Everyone was busy in the kitchen and didn't notice them. After Josy left, Greg went back into the kitchen to say his goodbyes.

"Where is Josy?" Sarah asked.

"I think she was feeling a little tired. She went back to her apartment."

"She walked?" Sarah could sense some tension, but didn't pursue it.

"Yes, she wanted some fresh air. I am heading home too."

"I thought you would stay with us tonight." Roger said.

"No, I've got an early morning. Good night all. I love you."

Greg left and the folks just stood there. Sarah said, "I think they had a tiff."

Mama H. said, "Don't worry, this happens. When the engagement is on, things get real, and the anxiety level goes up, that's when folks have some spats. They will be all right."

A few weeks later, Josy was looking out Greg's apartment window. It was a small one. You could not see much. His back deck was better. You could see Lake Ontario. The sunsets were beautiful.

"I don't know, Greg, Josy commented over her cup of chamomile and his cup of coffee, I'm starting to think your idea of a drag strip wedding wasn't as bad as I thought. All this wedding planning these last few months has been...frustrating."

"Well, the wedding really, is for the family. But everything will work out. We just have to remain as calm as we can."

"I know. It's just that with all the work hours we are putting in at the shop, and the running back and forth from the lake to home; it's a lot. My mom is really looking forward to all of it. But...I just want to get it over with."

"That's because you are a task oriented person. Weddings, as we have found, don't always lend themselves to a static list of things to do. They can change…all the time. We have no choice but to be a little flexible."

"Are you saying I'm not?"

"Hey, it's understandable. It's not like we're 20. We have established lives and know what we want. But if we need to, if it's too much right now, we could push the date back a bit."

"What?" Are you crazy? We have already booked the venue."

"Yes, but they have people change their dates all the time. We would not lose our deposit."

"So you want to wait."

"No, I'm not saying that, I'm just saying I am…open to the possibility."

Josy raised her voice. "Open to the possibility? What does that mean? If you have thought about not losing our deposit, it sounds like you're more than 'open to the possibility.' Are you backing out of our engagement?

Greg raised his voice to match. "Of course not. Don't overreact."

"Overreact?" Josy turned away and went out on the back deck. *Why am I so agitated?* She wondered. She sat there feeling the cool breeze off the lake. The night air was refreshing. She took in a few deep breaths. Greg had come out the door and offered her the rest of her tea if she wanted. She took it and said, "Thank you," but they didn't speak again that night.

The wedding date had been set for the following fall, a September wedding. Josy wanted a simple wedding, but had given in to her mom's desire to go all out. She loved her and wanted her to have the experience. Sarah and Harry never had a 'real'

wedding. They eloped on a weekend and never had a reception or party. They just went on with their lives.

But as Sarah got into all the planning, Josy was more nervous of all the expense her mom would encounter as well as Greg and herself. Most of the guests would be old friends of her mom's and Greg's parents. She and Greg would invite friends from work and a few others but the vast majority would be folks they barely knew.

There was a lot to plan and with all the work she was doing to get her detailing business afloat, it was all wearing on her nerves. But she was moving forward and pressing on. She had her mind set on the date; and as she found out, a year, really wasn't a long time to plan a wedding this big. So when Greg suggested waiting, pushing the date back, she actually agreed, but she would not admit it, because she had a fear of it all coming apart. So, the more she thought of pushing the wedding day back the more tightly she held on to it.

Up to now, they never had a fight. Not an out and out one anyway. But now she had not really talked to Greg for a week. At work, they had to talk, but only about work. She told him she needed some time. He went home to his place and she hers. He up at the lake and she back in town. It was like a wall came down between them. She didn't understand it, but it was there. She didn't want to be around him, which made her very uneasy now about the whole wedding thing. She had dinner with her mom on the Sunday following the 'argument' but they didn't talk about the wedding or Greg. Sarah had tried, but Josy shut her down.

"Mom, I just need some time. A week, maybe two. Okay? Let's talk about something else…anything."

After the first week and a half, she had an appointment with her counselor, Wendy. Josy talked about all the wedding plans, the changes the additions, the expense. She understood it was her and Greg's wedding, but she wanted to include her mom and Greg's mom too. Theresa had a tough life. Losing her daughter, this would be her only wedding. Making accommodations for the mothers was the right thing to do, but it also brought compromises that grated on Josy. Then the idea of pushing things back made her even more anxious. "It's my old battle with anticipation...you know, like the song says, ...it's making me wait."

Wendy listened to all of this and then asked this question, "How is your sex life?"

"What? What has that got to do with all of this?"

"I'm just asking the question. You don't have to answer, you don't have to say anything. But I want you to think about it."

Josy just sat there, thinking to herself. *Sex life? What kind of question is that? We have not done more than kiss. I think Greg is a virgin, I know I am. But what does that matter. If we both want to wait for our honeymoon...we've waited all these years so what are a few more months?*

Wendy interrupted Josy's thoughts. "Josy, it's not unusual for all the tensions to build up. And sometimes sexual tension needs to be addressed. It is a natural thing in young folks."

"Young? We're both 35! Is this feeling, a midlife crisis?"

"No, no. Believe me. I had that, when I was about 45. And yes, you are young. When you reach my age, you'll realize just how young 35 can be, or 45 for that matter. Now, have you and Greg been intimate? Again, you don't have to tell me, but if you have not, that tension may be part of what you're feeling."

Josy finally answered, "We are waiting for our wedding night."

"You and Greg decided that?"

"Well, not specifically, but it sure seems so. Greg has never made any advances that way."

"Well, if you both have agreed or do agree to that idea; great. But with that decision, you have to find a way to deal with the natural tension that is building as you spend time together and get closer and closer."

"How do we do that?"

"Well, I am not that kind of counselor, but, spending time in family groups or with friends helps, and there are resources I can refer you to such as..."

Josy didn't hear the rest. She drifted into thoughts of her and Greg together as husband and wife. She could feel her heart rate increase and her breathing quicken. The thought of the wedding night had been on her mind more and more as she was close to Greg at work or at one of their apartments. They would spend a lot of time in the evenings usually at Greg's place since it was near work. He had an extra room which he put a twin bed in for her. "I don't want to assume anything if you stay overnight." He had said. Their kisses were very passionate but never went further. Sometimes she wondered why Greg didn't go further, but she never said anything.

She never planned for this. All the years after graduation, she never thought about this. She was always wrapped up in her books and eventually her fantasy life as different women which in the end culminated with Lacey MacLean. But now it was real with Greg. Would she let him touch her intimately? She would like it. But would she allow it? She never, as of yet, had to answer that question because he never made an advance. But as she sat there, not listening to what Wendy was saying, she could only think of making love to Greg. It was too much. She jumped up from the chair.

"I need to go."

"Okay, our hour is just about up anyway. Just remember, if you know the basis for your anxiety you will be better able to handle it and move forward. Just like you did with the Abernathy incident. Right?"

Josy turned back from the door, and let out a big sigh, "Yes. And thanks again for all your help. See you next month."

"Okay, and if you need anything, just call me."

As Josy drove home she wondered about it all.

Should we not wait? How would I suggest that? I don't want to mess this up. What if I am not...good...in bed? What if Greg isn't? What does that mean anyway?

She said out loud, "God, I don't pray, I don't even know if you're there, but I could use some help here."

Just then a family of deer ran across the road. Josy put on the brakes and screeched to a halt narrowly missing the fawn. Her heart was racing again, but for different reasons this time. She pulled to the side of the road. She stewed in her thoughts.

Great! Thanks for that! I ask for help and you almost made me crash my Pinto Wagon! I could have killed that little...Bambi!

But as she watched the deer disappear into the brush, she had a thought.

Every wild animal makes love...naturally. They don't worry about it all. It just happens when it's time. Okay, okay...so maybe I won't worry about it either. Well, at least I am going to try not to. She rolled her eyes at herself because she knew her trouble with anticipation. *Me, not worry? That'll be the day.*

She then looked up...chuckled, shook her head and drove off.

◄ ◄►•◄ ►

Having a cup of coffee at Humphries Diner with Mama H. one Saturday, Josy talked about her and Greg's argument.

"I think it's just too much. I am having trouble turning my mind off from work. Even when we are choosing napkins and such. I keep thinking about what I have to do back at the shop. And so is Greg. He is not into choosing all this wedding stuff. He tries, but, it's clearly not his thing...you know...a drag strip wedding?"

Mama H. chuckled, and then said, "You asked me to stand up with you. And as your matron of honor I can help with the planning, so can your mom. We are there for you."

"Well, I want to ask you. But I'm not sure about Mom, and that's the problem. I don't want to leave her out. It's just that she gets so excited and the next thing I know, it's like she's taking over. So...but if I ask you and not her...it's...I don't know. I just don't want to hurt anyone."

"Hey, I can run a little interference there. If it seems like you're losing control, just give me a sign and I can butt in with a suggestion to break things up. We can do this. You don't have to do it all by yourself."

"I don't know."

"Hey, I seem to remember you asking, 'What would Lacey do?' Remember that?"

"Umm...yeah, but I don't see what that has to do with any of this.

"Well, do you imagine Lacey doing all the work to be an F....aah..."

"F-1 driver."

"Yes, thank you. She couldn't do it all by herself, could she? She had a team around her, right?"

"I suppose so."

"So, we are your team. Why don't we plan a time to get together, you, your mom, Theresa and myself. We can discuss all the wants and plans and especially what you want. And trust me, your mom will be happy for you no matter how big or small the plans. I'm sure Teresa will feel the same."

Josy agreed and she said she would call everyone to set up a day.

Chapter 4

The Ol' Gas Station

Josy, Greg and Charles Goodwin stood there, staring at the run down old gas station.

Josy turned to Charles, "Are you sure? He really meant for me to have this?"

"Yes, I am sure. We talked about this very thoroughly."

"This is...extraordinary! How could he do this? I don't understand."

Greg lifted Josy's hand to his lips and kissed it. "You know, you don't have to be extraordinary to do an extraordinary thing. You just have to say yes. Most, every good thing in this world starts with the word, Yes."

Josy gave Greg a sideways look. "Where did that come from? Are you a philosopher now?"

"I don't know. I heard it somewhere or maybe I read it in some magazine."

"It is a good saying." Then Josy smiled as she said, "If only you had written your wedding vows with the same poetic...ness"

Greg laughed, "Come on, they weren't really that bad."

Charles broke in, "Okay, so if you could just sign the document in the places I have marked...we can get this all settled. I have the keys. We can go inside and sign this. My uncle left this in a trust so all you have to do is sign. He even paid your trustee fees and I will get the documentation to the village and county. So all you have to do is sign."

Josy was in shock. It had been so long since she had set foot on this property. It had been a few different things over the years but never a gas station again. The tanks were taken out in the 80's and it had been painted a weird pink color for some head shop that was there...briefly...they were selling more than just tie-died tees. The owners were arrested and the shop closed down.

"I got some tie-dye shirts from here once." Greg said as they walked in to the office.

"Really? The one you wear at the shop sometimes? Did that come from here?" Josy asked.

"Yeah, It's one of my favorites. I like the Grateful Dead."

"Me too, Said Charles, Now, Josy, sign here, and here, and initial there." He had cleared the dust off the counter and set the documents there.

"Well, I don't know what to say, Josy said, If he, your uncle, was still here, I would say thank you. And I do thank you Mr. Goodwin for arranging it all. But still, this is...it's a bit overwhelming."

"It's okay, I understand. When he first asked me to do this I was, well, a little worried he had lost his faculties. But the more he talked, the more I knew this was his true wish."

"He didn't have to do this. If it's some kind of...I don't know..."

"Penance? Charles interrupted. No, this was...I think...well, he left a trust for my children too, he just adored them. In fact, he credits them for saving his life. And you, well, you...reminded him of his Laney. So, I think he wanted to leave something significant for you because of that, and also because of all you had been through."

"So…it is…penance." Josy was getting a little anxious about being 'paid off' for the trauma Mr. Abernathy had caused her.

"No, I really don't think so. You forgave him, he finally forgave himself. Listen, you should tell your mom about this. She may have some insight for you."

"What has my mom got to do with this?"

"Look…I have probably said too much, and I have to get to court, so…"

Josy just stared at him, and then gave Greg a questioning look. Greg nodded for her to go ahead and sign the papers which she did.

"Thank you and I hope you have good luck with this place. It certainly will need some work…for whatever you might want to do with it."

Charles left Josy and Greg standing there. They looked around a bit, Josy went into the area that used to be the garage. It had been renovated. The overhead doors were gone and a wall had been put up with shelving for merchandize. A floor had been put in over the cement one. It still had a faint smell of oil though. Greg had been checking out the old apartment which had not been touched.

"Hey Josy, come here" He said.

Josy came in and looked around. The paint had been pealing and fading, but she noticed it was the same colors from when they left the station so long ago.

"Wow, no one has lived in here? It's the same as the day we left…except for all the boxes and dust."

"I think it must have been only used for storage."

"Greg, I don't know what to think about all this. And what was that comment about Mom? I am confused."

"Well, you should…maybe…talk to her?"

Josy was looking around, as Greg was speaking. Then she sighed and said, "Yes, I, and *we*…should. After all, this is going to be ours." At that Josy gave Greg a peck on the cheek. He smiled and tossed her the keys which Charles had left on the counter.

A week later, Josy and Greg were at Sarah's house. Josy gave her mom a hug from behind as she was preparing lunch.

"Mom, I have been given a gift. And, well, it will belong to Greg and I once we're married."

Sarah turned around with a questioning look. "What kind of gift?" She took Josy's hand and they sat down next to each other. Greg joined them at the table as Josy explained. Sarah had a knowing look on her face.

"I kinda thought that might happen."

"How did you know, Mom?"

"Well, when we had to leave the gas station, I knew that made George quite happy. One day I saw him in town and he confronted me. It was not a pleasant conversation."

"What do you mean?"

"He said, well he said a lot of….uhh…he said that someday he would buy our place and burn it to the ground."

"What did you say to that?" Greg asked.

Sarah just shook her head and said, "What could I say? We were struggling to make ends meet and your dad was depressed over it all. I just broke down crying. I tried to hold it in. I didn't want to give George anymore satisfaction, but I could not hold back the tears."

"I'm so sorry, Mom." Josy said as she put her arm around her.

"It's all right, that was a long time ago. And look how things have turned out. He did not burn it or tear it down. Now I know why...He gave it to you!"

"Mom, Mr. Goodwin, you know, Mr. Abernathy's nephew, said you might know something...know why he left it to me."

Sarah suddenly got up. "I...well...I...someday...maybe...but not now."

"What do you mean?" Josy was really curious now.

"He gave it to you out of love and longing. That's all I will say right now. Please don't ask me any more. Please." Then Sarah left the kitchen for her bedroom.

Greg and Josy looked at each other not knowing how to react.

"Well, she'll tell you eventually. Right?"

"I don't know, it took her a long time to tell me the story of Laney and everything."

"It's all a bit overwhelming. What will you do with the station?"

"You mean what will *we* do with it? Right?"

"Well, It really is your decision, I will support you no matter what, and I will be happy to be your consultant," he said with a smile.

Josy sat down at the window seat and watched a flock of birds do a fly by. "Look, we need to talk about a few things. We should take a weekend away. Maybe we should head to the Falls."

"That sounds good. But can we spare the time?"

"I don't care. We need the time."

"Okay. Let's do it."

"I don't know what to do." Sarah said to Theresa.

"What to do about what? Could it be much ado about nothing?"

Theresa was actually 'full of it' herself. Greg got the funny bone, and the practical joking gene from both his parents. Theresa was very quiet but had a dry sense of humor. Sarah chuckled at her comment.

"I wish it was so 'Oh Juliet,' but alas it is too hard to tell."

Theresa laughed, "Bravo! Way to mix and match Shakespeare." Theresa took a sip of coffee, then took a breath and got serious. "Sarah, let me be your sounding board. Tell me." She reached across the table and touched Sarah's hand.

Sarah looked out Theresa's kitchen window. The snow was deep and the wind was howling. She was thankful for a hot cup of coffee and a warm kitchen. The tale to tell was so hidden for so long that she could hardly believe it was real herself. But she knew she had to get it out now. She steeled herself and began,

"Well, I say this to you in strictest confidence."

"You have my word."

"Has Josy told you about what happened many years ago with George Abernathy? How he and his wife Ellie lost their daughter Laney because of a mistake my husband Harry made on fixing his brakes and how he then grew in hatred and began stalking Josy...well, and then he scared her half to death at the gas station one night when we were getting dinner...how she was all alone with him while he was going crazy in a drunken rage?"

"Yes, Greg has filled me in."

"Well, now, she found out that George left her the old station. He bought it, you see, a while back and for years just let it sit there. He told me once that he was going to burn it down."

"That would have got him in a heap of trouble."

"Well, I think he meant he would just have it torn down. But he never did. I didn't know why. But now he's gone and left it to Josy...and...I...do...know why."

"You do?"

Sarah looked out the window at the snow, cold and frozen. That is how her throat felt. She did not want to speak. She just stared out the window.

"You can get a counselor, like I have." Theresa broke the silence.

"I know, but you're here, I'm here, I trust you."

Theresa began to tear up a little. Not many people besides her family ever took the time to get to know her, much less trust her.

"Thank you. That's the nicest thing anyone has said to me."

"Really?"

"Well, outside of my Roger, Greg and of course our Annie, most folks look at me, my skin, black hair and my nose and they just look the other way. I don't have many friends. My mother and her family were not happy with me marrying Roger. I wasn't welcome at their home for a long time."

"I'm so sorry. It's so hard to be lost to family."

"Well, I have always been a black sheep. I am not full blooded you know."

"Really? So what are you?...I'm sorry...that came out wrong."

Theresa laughed. "What am I? Good question. I am a Tonowanda Seneca, my mother is, as was her mother. This land we all live on was once all Tonowandas. The earth, the land is also our mother. So in truth, we are hers. Creator is our father and earth is our mother because we came from her."

Sarah interjected, "Wow, I never thought of it that way before. How interesting. But then, you said you were not full blooded."

"Yes, I am one half French or English, I'm not sure. My father gave me that blood."

"So you are like your mother. She married outside her people too."

"No. She wasn't married to that man if you could call him that. I say he wasn't even a human being. He was worse than a dog."

Sarah instantly understood. "I am so sorry. May I ask what happened?"

Theresa stared out the window now. There was a long silence again before she spoke. "My mom was taken from her family at the age of 8 to a school. These were like reformatories. They stripped the land away from us, our families, our language our dignity as a people. Our thousands of years of culture meant nothing to them. They said we were savages that needed to be saved."

"I have never heard about that."

"Of course not. No one talks about it. Some of the Nuns and Priests were very mean and strict. They beat my mom and others if they stepped out of line in any way. And then, when my mom was only 15...there was this handy man...he took care of the grounds and stuff like that. He caught my mom alone in the laundry and...he..."

"No!" Sarah interrupted. She then reached over and put her hand on Theresa's shoulder. "I...don't know what to say...I'm so sorry. Now I know why you called him a dog."

"Worse than a dog" Theresa said under her breath.

"So what happened when you were born?"

"My mom had escaped and managed to get back home and soon it was clear she was pregnant. My family hid her from the authorities and after a while they just stopped looking. My mom gave birth to me at our family home. As I grew it was clear I did not fit in with the rest of my clan. As a teen, I rebelled against everything and left. I got work on a farm with the pickers who traveled up from Florida. Many of them were descended from slaves. They understood rejection. I fit in with them."

"How did you meet Roger?"

"Well, that's another story. But what about you? You were going to tell me your story."

Sarah took a deep breath. "This must be what a confession is like and you are like my priest. I don't know if I can even say this."

"Take your time and only tell me if you really want to."

"It's just that it's been buried for so long. You see George and I...well, we have history."

"George Abernathy? The man who caused Josy and you all that trouble?"

"Yes, that George. You see, we had been friends before Harry and I married. I was younger, and I always had a big crush on him. Anyway...when Laney was a baby I would watch her for George and Ellie sometimes. We became, very close...too close. When I met Harry, I really needed to be away from George. Harry and I eloped on a bit of a whim. We started the gas station and were so busy. I thought I was over George. Then, later that year, I got pregnant. But it ended in a miscarriage. And, then two more pregnancies ended in a miscarriage. That caused a lot of stress on our new marriage. I was depressed...desperate. Harry became distant. Looking back I can see that it wasn't that he blamed me or didn't love me, I think it was that he was scared of getting pregnant again only to lose another. But the effect was the same. I became lonely.

I was over to Abernathy's a lot, baby sitting little Lane for Ellie who just started working nights. After working at the station all day, I would go over after dinner to take care of Laney. Well, George and I...I just adored him since I was a kid. You know what I mean? I thought I was past that...but, we were together for hours. We'd talk and laugh and share stories...have a little too much wine...and...well...I...I am so...ashamed. I became pregnant again during that time."

Theresa sat there for a moment. "So, you are saying Josy is not Harry's? She was really George's"

"I don't know for sure. We only...Sarah sighed...only one time. But...Josy...sure...did look a lot like Laney."

At that Sarah teared up and looked away. Theresa put her hand on Sarah's shoulder slightly rubbing it. They sat there, the afternoon sun bathing them in light through the window.

One Sunday afternoon, all the women gathered at Sarah's to go over wedding plans. It was better now that there was understanding of what Josy wanted and wanted for her mom and for Theresa. Greg sat in as well, but mostly he kept the coffee coming. The wedding was only 3 months away now and they all had just finished addressing the invitations. Mama H. had a Chaplain friend who agreed to perform the ceremony. They would get married in a beautiful old chapel on the lake. The reception would be at their favorite restaurant which was also a banquet facility. The wedding cake would be a carrot cake, Josy and Gregs favorite. Josy's dress was in the fitting stage along with Mama H.'s and the 'Moms' as they were calling themselves. They hit it off, Theresa and Sarah. Greg noticed and commented to Josy that this was the first time he saw his mom get close to someone other than his dad.

"Your mom and mine have really hit it off. I wonder how that happened?"

"My mom could befriend a rock, not that I am saying your mom is…" Josy blushed with embarrassment.

Greg just laughed "I am glad they are getting close."

As the evening was approaching, they all said goodbyes and headed home for dinner. Josy and Greg asked Sarah if she wanted company for dinner. She declined and said, "I am actually going to Theresa's for dinner. Your dad is out with his bowling buddies."

"Okay, well, have a good time." Greg and Josy got a double hug and their coats handed to them.

Josy and Greg sat in the car looking around at the old gas station.

"I don't know, Josy said, What will we do with this place? Just look at the windows…all cracked. There's so much to do just to make it weather tight."

"We can duct tape the window glass. Hey, remember what our old tech teacher said about trucks? 'A truck isn't really a truck until it has some duct tape on it.' I always kinda understood that."

Josy laughed. "This place is going to need a lot more than duct tape. And your truck doesn't have any duct tape on it."

Greg thought for a moment and then replied, "Well, my truck is still in training."

Josy sighed and just looked at him. "Well, as I said, this place is going to need a lot more than duct tape. Anyway, we don't have to do anything right away. We have time."

"Yes, the wedding...the wedding comes first, that's for sure. And besides, you're still getting your business off the ground. But we will have taxes to pay on this place."

"We'll figure it out." At that Josy gave Greg a kiss and they drove off to get dinner.

"My life is full of guilt." Sarah said as she sat with Theresa at dinner.

"I feel that too. So did my mom. Even though it wasn't her fault. Guilt is an awful task master. It sucks the life right out of us at times."

"But your mom and you had nothing to feel guilty about."

"My mom felt guilty for not being able to fight...ashamed, worthless. The life was sucked right out of her. I felt guilt over being the 'gift' of the rapist. I had a lot of mixed feelings about having children. And then, postpartum blues, as they say. And in my depression I just couldn't find a way to be present for my family."

"But that wasn't your fault."

"It doesn't matter. Depression and guilt...they don't care whose at fault. They just like to be in control. And many times I gave them all control because it seemed easier than stepping up to take control and responsibility myself."

"You talk about guilt and depression as if they are...I don't know...alive?"

"Well, it was an idea from counseling. A way to separate those feelings from myself. It helps."

"I've always avoided talking about my past because facing it all makes me depressed and feel bad."

"Depression makes us do crazy desperate things. But, not always bad things. I was so desperate to be present to Annie when she was dying, that I got help. I needed counseling and proper medication. I found out that my depression was not caused by my guilt only..."

"You mean, false guilt, don't you?"

"Yes, okay, but it was also my brain chemistry."

"Brain chemistry?"

"Yes, come to find out, I am not right in the head." Theresa let that statement sit for a moment...Sarah did not laugh. "Just a little joke...but I am missing certain enzymes or whatever and that causes or helps cause my depression. Medication helps. I am very thankful that I became desperate enough to get help and find all this out."

"Well, my desperations led me to do something with George that could have ruined everything. So when I got pregnant, we just did not speak. I had to stop babysitting for them anyway. That year, I know he suspected, but never asked. I certainly wouldn't say anything and besides, Harry and I...became intimate again, I am sure of that. But it's...it's, just that the timing was...I don't know...it's all so...aah..."

"Harry never knew?"

"How could I admit it to him? It would have ruined our marriage for sure. Then Laney died and the whole incident at the gas station happened...so it just, seemed best to keep it hidden. And I'm not sure if it will do any good to tell Josy now. Won't it do more harm than good to say anything? I am not sure why George told his nephew, well, he probably had to for the trust I guess. It's all so…hard. I don't know what to tell Josy…and she's asking."

"When I was young, I thought my mom would have done me a favor by saying she got pregnant from one of our young men. I would have been treated better. But then they would have wanted to know who…aah…some things just happen and that's that. We have to hold on to grace, don't we."

Sarah closed her eyes. "Yes, I suppose so. I guess I have held on to that…well, ever since Josy was born. It's all I have for what I did, well, besides the guilt…which is terrible. You know, I can never judge anyone…for long…I just look in the mirror and remember."

"My mom was raped. Terrible. But then I was born. Wonderful. At least that's what my grandma said when I was upset over being called a half-breed bastard. Even though she suffered so much having my mom ripped from her hands and taken away, she always pointed to the good."

"The good? Harry always treated me so good. I loved him too…it's just that…the memory…the dreams…it was not good for a long time. I just got used to the guilt I guess. And then there was Josy. She took my heart and wrapped it around her finger, as she did Harry's. She is the good…the grace…my Josy."

"I guess that is life, the good and the bad all mixed up together. What can we do?"

Sarah shook her head and looked out the window. "I don't know…I just don't know. How can I tell Josy George could be her…" Sarah stared at Theresa, then they both stared out the window.

At Niagara Falls, the weekend away was beautiful. The sun was shining over the waters and the spray was causing multiple rainbows. Josy and Greg just enjoyed each other's company and relaxed. No talk of the wedding, business or why the station was given to Josy. They just went to dinner, out for drinks and dancing. The line dance turned into a conga and Greg was behind Josy with his hands on her hips. As the slow dancing started they looked at each other with love and longing for what was to come. Body to body, swaying, light kisses. They could only think of one thing. Later walking back to their hotel, Josy leaned in close and whispered.

"Are we going to wait for our wedding night?"

Greg gave her a knowing look. "I...aah..."

"I'm sorry, am I making you nervous?"

They stopped and Greg turned to Josy.

"It's been...well...it's not easy waiting. But I was always told it would be worth it."

"Yeah, I was told that too. And I know all the reasons why we should wait. It's only a few more months and...it's the right thing..."

Greg grabbed her and they kissed.

Chapter 5

The Big Day

It was a rainy fall day. Leaves were all over the wet road as Greg hurried to get to the chapel. As he turned right on the road leading to the lake, he skidded into a car that was in the opposite lane. Hitting the passenger door he came to rest staring at a scared child in the back seat. He immediately backed up and then jumped out to see if the little boy was okay. The mother jumped out of her car too and they ran right into each other.

"I am so sorry!" Greg said standing there in his tux. "Are you all okay?"

"Please move! I need to get to my baby."

"Yes, yes, I am so sorry."

"You said that." The woman pulled the toddler out and looked him over and held him close.

"Is he okay? Do we need to call 911?"

"I think we should...just to be safe."

Greg got in his tow-truck and used the CB radio to call for help while the mother sat back in the car with the little boy in her arms. Folks from cars that had stopped, directed traffic around the accident. As Greg waited for emergency crews to show up he realized he was probably going to be late to the wedding. The chapel had no phone, no electricity. It was going to be a candle light service. But what could he do? After exchanging insurance information, the police and the EMTs arrived. They looked the young boy and his mother over. They were both fine. The car was drivable. Greg's truck had no damage.

Greg said to the woman, "I happen to own a body shop. I can fix this for you without getting the insurance company involved if you like."

"I...don't know. I should ask my husband."

"Well, you have my number and you see the sign on my truck. I fix cars for a living, but if you have your own mechanic, that's fine."

It took a long time for the police officer to fill out the report and issue Greg a ticket and by then it was already dark. When the officer finally finished, he commented on Greg's tuxedo. "Sir, are you in a hurry to get somewhere special?"

"It's my wedding day. And I am late."

"Where are you going?"

"The Landing Chapel, up on the lake."

"Follow me." Said the officer.

Josy was standing there in the doorway of the tiny room off the altar area. Sarah and Theresa were just outside asking Roger where Greg was.

"Well, he had to go to get something he forgot. He said he would be right back. But that was 20 minutes ago."

Mama H. was outside with the groomsmen asking the same question. They said that Greg ran out a while ago and jumped in his tow-truck, saying he'd be right back.

"Can you get a hold of him?"

"There's no CB here. That's all he has in his truck."

Mama H. was thinking about someone who might have a car

phone. But since Greg didn't have one the thought was moot. Mama H. went to the little room where Josy was waiting.

"Where could he be? I hope he's okay. I am a little worried. We should be saying our vows by now!"

"I'm sure he's okay." Mama H. said, as she stared out at the rain, which now was coming down hard.

"Did he stop to help someone who's car broke down? What if he got in an accident? What if he changed his mind and isn't coming?"

Theresa heard Josy's questions and came over, took her by the shoulders and looked her straight in the eyes. "Now don't you worry. My boy will be here. No matter what. He loves you. You know that."

"I know. I'm just...the people are all here...waiting... wondering what's going on. And the candles are lit, they're only going to burn for so long. Should we say something? Josy looked as water was bouncing in the entry way from the downpour. Aagh, this rain! And on my wedding day!"

Sarah spoke softly, "Lord, help my girl."

Mama H. spoke up, "Just take a deep breath. I'm sure he will be here as soon as he can." She then went to the front of the chapel and made an announcement that there would be a delay, and she asked the people to be patient and for everyone to sit tight.

As Greg followed the police car north he looked down at the bushings he had fashioned on chains. Each was polished and etched with his and Josy's names. He planned on making the gift as part of the toast he would give at the reception. A bushing was an important thing to a mechanic. It was used on axles and so many other areas. It was a guide, a stop, it could reduce friction or it could be threaded to join two rods or pipes. He planned on saying these were a symbol of that kind of joining in his and Josy's relationship. He had them in a nice box all ready for the moment. That's what caused him to leave the chapel. Standing in the vestry looking out the window over the lake, he suddenly realized he had forgotten the bushings. So he left and hurried to his apartment. But then he took that corner too fast…and crash! He knew he'd be late, and just hoped Josy would still be waiting. As he pulled into the chapel he waved a 'thank you' to the officer and saw Mama H. standing in the rain with an umbrella looking relieved, but a bit stern.

"Where have you been?" She said as Greg hurried to the door.

"Got into an accident" He said as he walked briskly passed her.

"What? She shook her head. Ah…Are you all right?" She said as she chased after him. Greg did not answer. "Okay…you're here, that's all that matters."

Greg rushed to the altar. He was a bit wet and his shoes and pants were a bit muddy on the bottom. His father pulled him aside and helped him dry off and clean up as Mama H. rushed off to tell Josy that Greg was back.

"I expect there is a story behind all this." Roger said as he straightened Greg's tie.

"I will tell you later. I'm just glad everyone is still here."

"Of course we are. We knew you'd be here. Now take a deep breath and relax. Nothing to worry about. It's *just* your wedding day."

They looked at each other and then chuckled.

"He's back!" Mama H. exclaimed.

Josy jumped up off the chair and gave her mom and Theresa a group hug.

"What happened to him?" Josy asked.

"I will let him tell you. Right now all that matters is that he's all right and he's here."

Just then, the chaplain walked in to see if they were ready. They shook their heads yes and got all lined up for the walk down the aisle.

Josy was escorted by Sarah who carried with her a picture of Harry. As she answered the question of who gives this bride to be wed, she said, "Harry and I do, with all our love." She then lifted Josy's vail gave her a loving kiss on the cheek and watched as she walked up to join Greg at the altar.

Josy looked Greg over with a questioning but relieved look and then whispered, "Is that a tear in your eye or just some rain drops."

Greg sheepishly smiled, but he didn't answer, as the Chaplain had already started.

When it came time for the vows it was Greg's turn to say his first. They had decided to write their own and Greg promised not to use the ones he had written the day of their engagement. But he held on to the note paper and pulled it out of his pocket intentionally showing it to Josy. She could see the big letters he used to write it and even though it was a bit wrinkled she knew instantly what it was. The words, 'WHEN YOUR BATTERY IS DEAD' could clearly be seen. She gave Greg a look...but he smiled broadly, wadded it up and gave it to her. She took it without thinking, looked at it and wondered, *what is this man of mine doing.*

Greg then said without looking at any paper, "In high school, I wanted to date you very badly. But I was always too scared to ask. And after we graduated, I thought I would just pop into the diner and ask, but again, I was too scared. It took me a long time to settle into life without the thought of you in it. Fear, shyness, kept me away from you for so many years and in the end it was only by chance that we met again. Chance or maybe some Divine intervention. But today, I am here, looking at you, getting married. I am not scared…I am terrified." At that everyone laughed. Then Greg continued, "I am terrified that I will not be all you want or need. But I am not afraid, 'cause we are together. I will always love you, no matter what. I take you as you are, to be my wife, my lover, and my best friend forever."

Josy just stood there with her own rain drops falling from her eyes. She said, "I can't say this without my paper. It's not that I don't know it by heart, but it's that I can't look up or I will lose it." Again everyone chuckled. Josy, with hands shaking a little, read her vows, "I was working at my old job at the DMV. It was a good job, but I knew I was not meant only for that. It took me a while before I learned how to just enjoy my 'mundane' work by helping people get through the papers and plates as best I could. At that point I was no longer looking to find my place, I was just making my current life and job my place.

That letting go of being disappointed in myself, let me be open to you, Greg. I too had settled into single life, but the day you came back into my life, deep down, I knew. I just knew we were meant to be together. Even though I did not know what that meant at the time. But then my place, my true place became clear, to be with you in business and in life.

"And now as we stand face to face, love to love, uniting as one, I am more sure than ever that you are to be my husband, just as you are, you are my lover, and my best friend forever." Then she unwrinkled the wadded paper of Greg's and said, "When our batteries die, we will recharge 'em for each other!" Greg just stood there and laughed. Everyone kinda chuckled but didn't know what that meant. Then Sarah, Theresa and Roger all laughed as they began to remember that day Greg read his crazy vows to them all. Greg announced, "It's an inside joke." Everyone laughed.

The Chaplain broke in and said, "Now folks, let us have the rings please." Josy and Greg just laughed all the more, remembering the balloon ride with the gum-ball ring. They tried to stop but the more they did, the more they laughed and just when they seemed under control, they looked at one another and broke out laughing again.

Finally the Chaplain took the rings from the best man and just started the ring ceremony. Josy and Greg managed to compose themselves and get through the ceremony without laughing anymore and then, the final words were said, they kissed and everyone cheered as they floated along down the aisle, barely hearing the words being said by the Chaplain, until she said "... for the first time, Mr. and Mrs. Greg Watkins."

The reception was a lively affair with music and dancing and all the usual festivities of dollar dances, bouquet tossing and such. At dinner, Greg made a toast and pulled out his bushing-rings each on a chain and placed his on Josy's neck and she in turn placed the one with her name on Greg's neck. "With these bushings, you were late to the wedding," she said. Greg answered, "Yes, that's true, I had forgotten them and went back to my apartment to get them. Then in the rush to get here I had a minor accident. Everyone is fine, just a dent in the door of the other car. I would have been even later, but the police gave me an escort all the way to the chapel. And I was so glad you waited, Josy."

"Well, I was a bit worried, but you made it. So here's a toast to my 'late' husband." Everyone lifted their glasses and toasted. Then spoons started tingling the glasses and Greg gave Josy a big kiss.

"Now, said Josy, I have some more vows to read." She then read the rest of Greg's original vows, and everyone laughed. Then it was time for the father-daughter dance and Roger stepping in for Harry. He told Josy, "I am so happy that you have blessed our family with your love for our Son. We prayed long and hard for him to find that certain someone. And here you are! Thank you."

Josy just gave Roger a big hug and then danced with her mom. Greg was dancing with Theresa too, and then the four of them came together and formed a circle. It wasn't long before Roger joined in and then a few more people got up and joined the circle swaying back and forth to the music. After a while they all sat down and had cake.

Josy and Greg had no trouble smashing cake into each others faces, laughing and enjoying the moment as pictures were taken. And all the usual photos of family groupings were then managed by the photographer and by that time, Josy and Greg were ready to go.

As rice was falling, they jumped into the Pinto Wagon and headed off...they told no one where they were going. That was one thing Josy planned by herself. Even Greg did not know. It would be a surprise. As they left in the dark downpour it was slow going on the midnight rural roads; but that didn't matter because they were together. Josy remembered the ride north and her little jingle, *Greg and me and the Pinto make three,* and she chuckled to herself.

Meanwhile, Greg was yawning.

"Hey, wake up buddy!"

"Ahh, I'm sorry, but that wine has made me very sleepy."

"You can't poop out on me on our wedding night."

"Zzzzz"

At that Josy gave him a punch in the arm. Greg just laughed, reached over and gave her a kiss. "Really, I am tired though. Where are we going?"

"I'm not telling. That's what you get for your kidding."

"Hey what's that smell? It's like a rose garden in here."

"Never you mind, Mr. Watkins."

Now Greg was curious. He looked around and even though it was dark, he could see some curtains in the back of the wagon covering the windows and the back seat was flat and covered with what looked to be a mattress and blankets. As they pulled into an RV Park he realized what Josy had planned, but didn't say a word.

As they parked in their spot Josy said, "So...we aren't tenting tonight."

"No, I didn't think so. It is a bit wet."

"Way back when we met, again, and I was driving my car, I had a thought. '*Me and you and the Pinto make three*' or something like that. Anyway, I decided our first night together should be right here in the back of our car. It was our shared labor of love that restored this baby and now...well...why not?"

Greg shook his head and chuckled a little. He wasn't quite sure Josy was not kidding to get back at him for all his pranks. But as he looked at her, he could tell she was serious. "Now, I thought I was a kidder...but you're not kidding, are you? Well, why not?"

Then Josy turned the key to the 'on' position and turned on the radio. She had rigged up all blue Christmas lights to the cigarette lighter port. There was champaign and glasses in the back, plenty of pillows and blankets and satin sheets.

"In the morning we can drive off into the sunrise again." Josy said as she climbed in the back of the wagon.

Greg got out of the front seat walked to the back hatch and lifted it up to get the full view of the 'honeymoon suite.' "When did you do all this?

"You know, in between things."

"It's really great. I would have never thought of this"

"Well, like I said, I had this thought of you and I making love right here in my car way back when, and even though I passed it off as childish, the thought kept coming back to me. And since we haven't done anything like that...up 'til now...I guess I wanted to. Do you?"

"Oh yes."

Greg jumped in and closed the hatch.

In the morning, it was cold. Greg jumped up front to turn the car on, but of course, the battery was dead. Josy just laughed. "Just like ol' times."

Greg sighed, "Well, like I promised... 'When you battery is dead...'"

Josy cut him off, "You'll jump me."

It was a while before they got out of the car.

Later, they asked the park owner if anyone there could give them a jump. The owner was Lucy. She sat in the park office and said, "Well I'm not surprised. You were, shall we say, rocking that car all night." Greg and Josy got red faced. "O I wasn't snoopin' or nothin'...and you're the only campers here so it's all good. Just having fun witch-ya."

She knew this was their first night of their honeymoon and had coffee waiting for them along with some doughnuts. They sat in the park office and laughed as Josy told Lucy how they met.

Lucy said, "So this is kinda appropriate to need a jump as you go off into your new life together. Glad we could help. My husband will be around with the truck and cables. Now, you know, check out was at eleven...and I should be charging you for another night. But, since you remind me of Joe and me when we were young...well, anyway good luck and God bless you two."

She then gave Josy a wink. Josy nodded and said, "Thank you so much for this. I know it's the end of the season and all but I can tell you, this made our honeymoon extra special. And you know why. Thanks again."

With that, they were off heading northwest into the *afternoon* sun.

Chapter 6

Complications

Greg got the call at 6 in the morning. He was getting ready to go into work as Josy finished showering. His whole building was engulfed in flames. He yelled to Josy as he rushed out the door, "Josy! Our body shop's on fire! Meet me there."

Josy hurried up and got dressed. She hopped into her Pinto and rushed off to meet Greg. As she pulled in, it was clear, this was bad. Greg was standing there in shock as she joined him. Arm in arm they watched as the firemen worked to quell the flames. It was not easy with all the oil and other flammable liquids that were present. It was fortunate this was not a gas station as those tanks could have been involved. But the whole body shop, along with the detailing shop would be a total loss.

"We have insurance." Josy said with a sigh as she hugged Greg.

After the honeymoon, Josy and Greg focused on the business. 12 hour days sometimes 7 days a week were common. They worked hard at making it all a success. But because they loved the work and doing it all together, they were happy. And when things got caught up and work was slow, they would disappear in the Pinto for a day or two. And they did get a tent...eventually.

At Sarah's house having a Sunday dinner, she commented about how busy they were. "Now you two can't forget to take time to be thankful and it wouldn't hurt to look up now and then and say a prayer."

Josy thought back to the only prayer she could remember saying...that day on the road when she almost hit the deer family. *I guess it all worked out. So maybe someone was looking out for me. Is that God?*

Greg saw Josy was in thought. "We do, in our own way Mom." He began calling Sarah, 'Mom' after the engagement was announced. Sarah loved it. She always wanted a boy and a girl. But she never got pregnant again. So Greg addressing her that way was nice.

"I'm glad you do. Prayer is a way to maintain peace and humility. It is putting faith ahead of yourself and your day. It will help you plow through the snows of life." She was looking out the window at Greg's truck when she said it.

"Speaking of that, I do need to go plow out the parking lot at work before tomorrow morning."

Josy was called back from her thoughts. "Yes, we need to go, Mom, and thanks for dinner."

"My Cuda is gone." Greg said as he looked at what was left of his body shop and Josy's detailing business. "I should have brought it home instead of the truck."

"But you will need your truck now, more than ever. You can get another Cuda, dear."

"A '72? Not many of those left around...here, anyway."

"Yeah...I guess that's true. I'm so sorry honey."

"Well, the one good thing is that it was a slow week, there

was nothing else in my bays, and you got the last of your detailing done before this mess."

"O No!"

"What?"

"Lucy and Joe's boat was in there. I was going to recover the seats. Now what?"

"You didn't tell me. When did they bring it over?"

"Saturday night, just before I drove home. It was last minute, they wanted to get it here before the snow storm."

"Well, we'll have to talk to our insurance agent and see how much of this is covered."

"You don't know?"

"Well, I think I pay for coverage of vehicles stored, but I don't know if we got a rider for your detailing shop. I can't remember."

"O yeah, I was there when your were talking about that, did we?"

"Well, I guess we'll find out."

"I gotta call Lucy. But what are we going to do about the jobs coming up?"

Greg stood there just staring at the mess. Finally he sighed and said, "Well, we've got the old gas station."

It was a mad rush to revamp the old gas station to use as a temporary work place while the insurance came through for the rebuild of Greg and Josy's body and detailing shop. Greg's employees all worked hard cleaning and remodeling. They wanted to help and were thankful to have a paycheck. Most of Greg's regular patrons were understanding and promised to stay with him. But is was a good two months before he could even begin to take on body work. Josy could not do any detailing work and would not be able to for a while. So she worked along side everyone else in getting the old gas station presentable and functional.

As she was painting the office area and the apartment, many memories came flooding into her mind. Dinners after exhausting days of work. Card games and stories. Laughter and tears. As she helped mount the new overhead doors, she remembered that night when George Abernathy terrorized her. The thought of him giving her this place was still very puzzling. She needed to ask her mom again, why his nephew said she would have more insight into this unusual gift.

One day as they were pulling up the wood floor to get down to the concrete, Josy began reminiscing about being there, with her dad and mom working. So many memories flooded into Josy's mind. She went into the old apartment and began looking around and remembering their lives so many years ago in this cozy place. Her mom always made it homey. Josy was looking through the closets and spotted an old box laying there behind some bags of refuse. She picked it up, opened it, to find some of her dad's Christmas ornaments. That brought back so many memories and she just sat down right there on the dirty floor and cried. Pulling out the ornaments one by one, remembering when she and her dad bought many of them. Or when he would surprise her mom with one on a birthday dinner. Her mom would just shake her head and smile at his childish ways when it came to Christmas.

Josy thought to herself, *No matter how hard life was, he never lost that...that...that joy... it was just pure joy. I have known that too, now, with Greg.* She then looked up and said a little thank you to her dad for giving her that experience of his joy. *The day*

72

you left us, was the day I lost that joy. It took me so long to find it again. Thanks Dad.

Tears were still flowing down her cheek when Greg found her. "Everything okay?"

Josy jumped up, wiped the tears away with her dusty hand. "I found this."

Greg pulled his dirty rag and tried to clean her face while asking, "What is it?"

"Christmas ornaments. My Dad's...well ours, but ones that he bought. Some of them I helped him pick out. They bring back a lot of memories." Josy then spied the dirty rag. She chuckled a little, "Ah...you are probably not helping my dirty face with that."

"Umm...no. I guess not. Let me go get something better."

"Okay, I will just sit here a while." Greg pulled up an old chair for her.

The rebuild of the garage by the lake was not going well at all. The money was there from the insurance, but building codes had changed, and there were environmental factors. The clean up and demo was not even allowed to happen yet. Time was ticking and Greg was itching to get back to work. Everyday it seemed there was another obstacle.

One day as they were picking through the remains of the fire, Josy said, "You know, we've got the old gas station fixed up fairly well. How much more would it take just to move the business there? And would you be okay with that?"

"Well, I would miss the lake, and you would too, but it's not that far of a drive on a weekend. But what about our apartment? It might be a bit much to make the drive everyday."

"You know, the apartment in the old gas station is not much smaller than ours. Why can't we fix it up and move in there?"

"Hmm...that would be...okay I guess. Although, is it wise to live on top of our work?"

"Are you kidding? We practically live here as it is, aah I mean lived here...as it was." They both gave out a big sigh.

"We always drive home at night."

"So we will drive around the block a few times after work."

Greg laughed. "Well, let's think about that. We'd have to sell the property up here, but who's going to want a burned out shell of a garage, not to mention all the EPA complications?"

"I will tell mom and she will tell Mama H. and they will pray."

"Really? You're asking for prayer?"

"Yeah, I don't know, I guess I have some faith that if it's meant to be, it will be. And besides, being there at the old gas station in our old apartment and remembering how mom used to make it so homey...I...well, maybe I can too. And I'm sure there is someone who will come along and...want this...this..."

"Mess."

"I didn't want to say it. All the blood, sweat and tears you have put into this place. It's just so sad."

The Ol' Gas Station was now the official name of Greg and Josy's place. It wasn't as big as the shop by the lake but they were making the best of it. They were waiting on a permit to put an addition on to set up Josy's detailing shop. Josy had asked her mom for prayers, which was a bit weird for Josy, but Sarah just agreed without making a big deal of it. She did mention it at the house over lunch to Mama H., who wasn't that surprised.

"You know from experience that sometimes as we get older faith is something that springs up in us humans."

"Well, that's certainly true of you and me. For me it was..." Sarah stopped there. Mama H. could see in Sarah's face that she could not finish that sentence. So she picked up the conversation.

"Yes, I guess it took the death of my son to shake me out of my...my...just busy...busy...life. I was so matter of fact about everything. At the diner I had to be on the top of my game. David's death took the life and everything right out of me. It was only then that I was open to God, even if it was to scream at him."

Sarah was hesitant to say anything. Only Theresa knew of Sarah's guilt over her tryst with George Abernathy. It was after she was pregnant that Sarah really felt scared over what could happen if this child was George's and if Harry found out. The fear and anxiety was overwhelming. Back then when she knew she was pregnant, that is when Sarah began praying to herself in earnest. *Lord, if you are there, I need help. I am scared. I know I have made a mistake. George did too, but I am the one who's pregnant. I will probably lose this baby just like I have the others before. And maybe that would be what I deserve. So...I think that's best anyway.*

The day she started bleeding, she figured this was it. But then, Harry rushed her to the hospital. A week later she was home, but then the tragedy of Laney's death was such a blow. The guilt was even worse. If this pregnancy went to term...she and Harry would have a new baby while George and Ellie just lost their beautiful little girl. And this new baby could be...probably was...George's too. It was just too much. Many thoughts invaded her mind. *I should have bled out and died. It's what I deserve.*

Sarah's mom had given her a little book when she was a

teenager. It was a book of circumstances and bible verses to go with each. One day while on bed rest before she gave birth, she remembered it, found it and opened it. She found her finger resting on these words:

When you are scared, read Psalm 121; Matthew 11:28; and 1Peter 5:6-7

Sarah got up very carefully and ambled to the dresser where her old Bible was. She looked up the passages and read them. Then again, out loud. She felt comforted. All through the last weeks of her pregnancy she read those three scriptures over and over. When it was time to go to the hospital she made sure she brought the Bible with her. Harry asked why. Sarah said, "I need that right now."

Mama H.'s words jolted Sarah from her thoughts. "Scream at God? I was cowering in fear."

"What? You were afraid of God?"

"It's a long story...one I'm not ready to tell you. Maybe someday."

Mama H., being a chaplain knew when to pry and when to leave it be, which she did.

Sarah just sat there remembering how that little book introduced her to faith. She never went to church much, but that Bible became her companion and little Josephine was her salvation. The joy she brought to Sarah's life just overshadowed all the guilt and fear. Sarah finally understood the word grace. She held it in her hands everyday, fed this grace and nurtured it. Josephine was her grace. And as Josephine gave way to Josy, Sarah just basked in the grace she had been shown. She cherished the forgiveness she felt. Even though she kept the secret of her and George's tryst, she felt okay about it because she had this beautiful young girl and would not do anything to harm her life, which revealing this secret could do.

And when George terrorized Josy that day many years ago, Sarah knew it was more than just the fact that Harry's mistake led to the accident. She could understand his sorrow and longing for Laney as he stared at Josy. When Ellie died, George began sending Josy little notes with words like, 'be a good girl' or 'you are strong', but it really upset Sarah. She hid them from Josy and Harry. They were tucked away in an envelope in the back of her lingerie drawer. She didn't know what to do. She thought about burning them, but then she thought of George's obvious loss and longing, and that thought made her keep them. But she wasn't about to let those notes disrupt her, Harry and Josy's lives. She was so scared when George came to the gas station that night and the subsequent drive by; so afraid he would say something that would reveal their secret. When she and the sheriff confronted him, Sarah almost said something to him alone, but they had never talked about it openly and she didn't know how to begin. George was so sorry and humbled about his behavior it didn't seem to be the right time anyway. And then, George got help and sobered up, so it seemed like George and God were keeping the secret too. She felt God understood. And as the years past, it was something she just didn't think about, until just lately.

Why did George tell his nephew? Was it really necessary? Is this his parting dagger at me? She wondered.

Mama H. saw that Sarah was preoccupied. "Maybe we can talk again. I have to head up to the hospital."

"Oh, okay. I'm sorry I am in wonderland." They said their goodbyes, Mama H. left and Sarah went to the window seat and just stared out at the trees and birds and wind blown branches. She wondered again, *Should I tell Josy?*

It had been five years since moving into the Ol' Gas Station and things were running smoothly. The apartment took a while but was fixed up nicely and the addition for Josy's detailing shop was completed a year after the fire. As it turned out, there was a corporation interested in the land where Greg's original shop was. Josy was able to find a boat that was the same as the one lost in the fire. Lucy was very understanding.

Greg was still looking for a replacement for his Cuda but so far had not found what he wanted. But overall things were good. Greg and Sarah hired more help to keep up with demand and it also gave them a little time off. One time as they were up at the lake, at their favorite restaurant, Josy looked at Greg and said, "I never thought I would hear myself say this. But since watching our sponsored children grow up, seeing them develop through the letters and pictures…I was wondering…how do you feel about having children…now?"

Greg sat back and took a moment to answer. "I say…Yes!"

"I'm almost 40…and I know my mom's history with miscarriages…so…"

"So adoption? I'm all for it. There are so many children who need parents."

"I love you…you read my mind."

"Well, we do think alike on most things."

"So how do we start?"

"Well, I was reading in this magazine…"

"As always…"

"Yeah, well, there are Korean babies available."

"It probably won't be simple, will it?"

"No, the article I read said it could take a while. But you and me...we can do it."

"This will complicate things. But, all right, let's do it! And let's tell mom and your parents and see what they have to say."

"We'll tell Mama H. too, she may have some connections to agencies."

There were many exciting and long conversations about this adoption process. It took a whole year before Josy and Greg were approved. When that final approval came through they all had a big party. It now was a matter of getting passports, visas and all the paperwork before they could fly over and be introduced to their new baby. Would it be a boy or girl? They wouldn't know until the final approval on the Korean side.

One evening when Josy, Greg and Sarah were having a BBQ at the Watkins home, looking over adoption literature, Sarah's face drooped and she fell off her chair. The stroke affected her whole left side. Though she survived, it was not looking good. Josy immediately moved into her mom's house and took care of her. Mama H. and Theresa also helped with Sarah's care.

This was taking all of Josy's energy and she and Greg had to make some hard decisions. First, Josy would have to step back from the business. Second, the baby. Could they go through with it at this time? Should they put it off? Could doing that jeopardize the whole process?

Sitting by her mother's side, Josy moved close to her mom's ear. She was thinking, *We don't know what to do about our little baby whoever she or he may be. I will never neglect you mom. It's just I don't want to lose this chance either.* But what she said was, "Mom, I love you and I know you can hear me…please pray for Greg and I. And please come back to us."

A week later, Mama H. was called in. Sarah had become lucid but her body was shutting down. Everyone gathered around as Mama H. led them all in an end of life ritual. Josy sat there with her mom and Sarah just beamed with love as she gazed upon Josy's face. She motioned for Josy to lean in, and said in a raspy voice, "My grace. You are my grace, Josephine, my baby, my grace."

Josy just cried. Then her mom looked up and said a little louder, "Harry."

They all stood up and stared at Sarah. Then she closed her eyes and didn't say another word. The next day she was gone.

Here I am again. In this window seat. Just like at Dad's funeral. What I am going to do without you Mom? Greg sat beside Josy and put his arm around her. They looked out at the summer day. The greens and yellows, the sun and the flowers…the white fluffy clouds. It was a perfect day, but for Josy, it was a day with a big gaping hole in it.

Three days later a notice came. There was a new born baby girl available and waiting. The adoption agency had set a date in two months for Josy and Greg to fly to Korea to bring their new baby home.

Weeks passed, but Josy wouldn't leave the house. She was preparing a nursery but mostly she just wandered around the kitchen or would sit at the window seat with coffee or tea. The memories were so palpable. She didn't want to be away from her mom's presence here. Greg went to work, came home and made lunch, went back to work, came home and made dinner. He made all the arrangements for travel. He didn't press it, but he began to worry that she would slip into a depression. Memories of his mom's depression made it become foremost on his mind. How could they start as new parents if Josy was in this state of mind?

He invited his parents and Mama H. over for dinner one Saturday. They all sat and talked of the new little girl and all the plans, while Josy remained silent. Josy got up from the table and went to the window seat. Roger looked at Mama H., but she looked at Theresa, who sighed and got up to go to Josy.

"My dear Josy, may I listen a while?"

Josy was taken back a little. Theresa was never this forward with her. And what did that mean? 'Listen a while?' So she kind of shrugged and nodded yes. They sat there for a long time, Theresa just being there not even touching Josy. They looked out into the night and watched the stars twinkle. Finally everyone was in the room just sitting and being silent. Josy suddenly started to cry. Greg came over knelt down and put his hand on Josy's knee. She looked at him and said, "I think mom gave up too early." Greg had a stunned look on his face but said nothing. Then Josy got up and said it louder. "Mom gave up!"

"What do you mean, my dear? Mama H. asked in a quiet tone.

"O Mama H., it's all my fault."

"What do you mean?" Greg asked.

"She knew me so well. I asked her to stay, but I was worried about her recovery taking all my time and maybe messing up the adoption. She could read me, she knew what I was thinking. She gave up so we could move on!"

With that Josy went into her bedroom and slammed the door. She couldn't stop thinking about it. She paced and paced. Every knock on the door was ignored. She pushed the chair against the door knob and sat down on the bed.

Everyone just sat there, not knowing what to do. Mama H. led them all in a prayer. Greg went and sat by the bedroom door, told Josy he was there and eventually nodded off. The next morning they all got coffee. There was not a sound coming from the bedroom and they all began to worry. Greg went to the door and knocked loudly. "Are you okay? Josy! Honey! Please answer me!"

Josy moved the chair, opened the door and flatly said, "Here look at these." She then went back to the bed and laid down.

Greg looked at the envelope. Inside were the notes the George had written to Josy many years ago. Hidden all this time. "What is this?"

Josy stood up and spoke loudly, "I don't know. I don't understand. Why would George Abernathy send me little.... aagh...love notes?" She began pacing back and forth as she spoke. "What kind of deranged man was he? And why does my mom have them? Why did she hide them? Did Dad know? What the hell?"

By then the noise of the conversation brought Theresa to the door. She cautiously walked in and said, "I think I'm done listening."

Josy was now at the Ol' Gas Station apartment and would not go back to her mom's house. It was only two weeks away from going to Korea and she was so angry with her mom she was beside herself. Hearing what Theresa had to say was agonizing. *She would tell Theresa but not me? Really? Why Mom? How could you keep this...THIS!...from me? How can I become a mother right now?* These thoughts just kept spiraling in her mind and soul. It was too much. She got into the Pinto and peeled out of the shop. Greg saw her go and realized where she was headed. He got into the truck and followed her all the way to the lake.

He parked a little way away and watched as she screamed at the lake, pounded the car and then sat there...and then got up and waded for a while. Then she spotted him. He got out of the truck and stood there waiting to see her reaction. She stared at him for a moment and then ran at him full out. He didn't know what she would do, but whatever was coming, he steeled himself for it.

Then Greg could see her face. She was crying and her arms opened up. He ran toward her and they embraced falling to the sand and grass. Tears flowing and tightly hugging him; Josy said, "I'm sorry."

"You have nothing to be sorry about."

"I have been so screwed up, and angry."

"It's okay. I love you. And I understand. You've had to take in a lot...all at once. How could you not..."

"Go crazy?"

With that she kissed him over and over. They sat there for a long while. Then Greg said, "Should we talk to a counselor?"

"No. Yes. Maybe, but first I want to talk to your mother."

Theresa opened the door to her house. Josy was standing there with Greg right behind. They hugged and went in to sit down at the kitchen table. Roger was there having a morning cup and offered one to them. They accepted. As Roger got up, he let out a little fart. He chuckled and said, "Excuse me. That was an unauthorized puff." They all laughed. Theresa quipped, "That's just part of getting old. You lose more and more control of your body."

Theresa could see the stress on Josy's face. "Come my dear, you and I can go in the living room. You boys stay here while we girls talk." She and Josy sat down and Theresa told Josy how her mom had come to reveal the secret to her. Theresa also related all that she had been through and how in her mind it all had the terrible and the wonderful all mixed up. "Now I have never told anyone. Not even my Roger and certainly not Annie or Greg. Well, I did tell my counselor of course."

Josy asked, "Why?"

"Well, when I was young, but old enough to understand, my mom told me. And I was not shy in those days. I told one of my friends who told another and another. The looks folks gave me made it clear...I was not wanted...a half-breed born of rape. That's when I turned inward. I never spoke of it again...at least not until I told your mom."

"Why did you tell her?"

"Because she needed to hear my story so she could open up about hers. I, at least had my counselor. But she had not told a soul. She kept her and George's secret all those years. That guilt takes a toll. You were what kept her...alive and living."

"I was her grace...that's what she whispered to me."

"Those two in the kitchen...they are my grace. As was Annie."

Josy suddenly remembered what Charles Goodwin said about his kids being what saved George's life. *They were his grace...*She thought...*children...what a gift they must be.*

With that they sat there silent for a while longer. Greg and Roger were in the kitchen talking and chuckling about little things, while making pancakes and bacon. The smells wafted in and roused their appetites.

Theresa got up and reached for Josy's hand, "Come on let's eat."

The plane ride to Korea was long. They arrived in Seoul at six in the morning. Jet lagged and tired, they slept until the late afternoon. The adoption agency had set up the introduction for the next day at Noon. It was hard for Josy and Greg to wait, and that evening, the anticipation was getting to be overwhelming, for both of them. The good thing was that they were kept busy by the agency and given a tour of Seoul and dinner. But sleeping that night was useless. They sat up talking about names and dreams for their new arrival. The shock of her mom's secret was still pretty fretful for Josy and they talked about that a lot as well.

"I'm sorry, I don't mean to bring a dark cloud over this. I should focus on the baby."

"No, don't do that to yourself, Josy. Listen. There is no way for you to process that your father could have been George Abernathy...not in a few weeks anyway. But there is something we can do. They have DNA tests nowadays. Maybe we can find out for sure."

"How would that work?"

"Well, do you think your mom kept a lock of your dad's

hair? I read that would be all you'd need. Or, maybe, some from George. I don't know. But I think it would be worth a try."

Josy didn't answer but wondered about it. She sat there trying to think of the possibility of her mom keeping a lock of hair from her dad. And if so, where it might be. The thoughts of that hunt kept her mind busy enough to nod off to sleep.

The next day, they sat there in the waiting area of the hospital. The lady from the adoption agency was Lee Lyn and translated for them what was said, but Josy didn't hear much. She was focused on the little nose and black hair sticking out of the blanket. The little baby girl was wrapped in a bright pink blanket. As the nurse gave her to Josy, Greg moved in close and they both just stared in the little face of their baby girl. Tears of joy just streamed down their faces and Greg gave Josy a tight hug and kiss on the cheek. Then he touched the baby's nose with his finger and said, "Boop." Josy just beamed and cooed away to her. She sat down and said, "I can't take my eyes off you...you're so...beautiful."

Greg and Lee Lyn finished all the release forms and they all headed for the taxi. They would fly home that very night. But one more form had to be filled out.

"What is the name please?" Lee Lyn asked.

"Ahh, we still haven't decided...I think?" Greg said sheepishly while looking at Josy for some help.

Josy looked up from the baby, gave out a loving sigh and said, "Grace"

Chapter 7

Time Flies

"The DNA results are here, Josy. They just came in the mail. Here, you have to open it." Greg said as he passed the envelope to Josy.

"Here, take Gracie." She handed the baby to Greg and slowly opened the letter. She read it silently and then looked up at Greg and smiled. Then they both gave out a sigh of relief.

Sitting at the window seat with her sixteen year old Grace laying on her lap napping was not an unusual thing for Josy these days. They had moved back into her mom's house after they had come back from South Korea. They needed the space and Josy was not as upset about it all anymore. The day she met Grace was the moment that washed away the terrible feelings she had for her mom. Greg asked her on the plane ride home, "Why the name, Grace? We never had that on our list."

"It just seemed right." Was all Josy would say. But when Theresa met the baby for the first time, she knew. Josy and her just exchanged knowing glances as Greg announced her to everyone there, "This is Grace Sarah Watkins!" It was quite a reception when they got back. All the family and their employees were there to celebrate their arrival.

When Josy and Theresa were alone, Theresa said, "So, little Grace, is...your grace...she has become that for you?"

"O yes. The moment I saw her, I don't know…it was pure love and joy all wrapped up in…grace. All the anger…just vanished. I understood what mom said to me as she died…that I was her grace. So, what else could I name this little one?"

Now this beautiful girl was going to be getting her driving permit. As Josy sat there caressing her long black hair Grace woke up and looked out the window as the birds were dancing away on the wind. "Look, Mom, see how the birds just dance. I love watching the birds."

"So do I my dear, so do I."

Grace was home from college one Thanksgiving weekend and took Josy aside. "Mom, I…hope you don't get upset…but…I think I want to find my birth parents…I mean, if it's even possible. I don't know…it's just been on my mind a lot lately. I've talked to friends at school from overseas and even Africa. They talk about their homes and traditions. It makes me wonder about my Korean heritage…and my birth parents. I mean…you're the best Mom ever…and Dad is…I'm sorry if this hurts you…I hope…"

Josy just hugged her tight and said, "I know, my dear, I know."

"You do?"

"Yes, I know what you're going through. I have been there."

"You have? But you're not adopted."

"Well, it's a long story, but…"

"But what?"

"I was going to say, 'someday I'll tell you.' But, no, now is a good a time as ever."

And Josy told Grace all about the Abernathy tale and how she finally found out that she was her daddy's girl. She found that lock of hair in her mom's picture diary. An album hidden away in her closet with pictures of Josy when she was a baby. And on a page were three locks of hair. Each in its own little baggie. The name of who's hair it contained was just above each baggie. The day she found that, Greg immediately took them and got the DNA testing started.

"You were only one year old when we got the letter. It was just such a relief to know I was my daddy's girl, not George Abernathy's. My DNA matched my father's. It is different for you, but the wanting to know...I understand."

Grace took it all in and went to the window seat. Looking out with a cup of green tea, her preferred drink, she remembered all the books her mom read to her here. It became their spot for books and talks. As Josy came and sat beside her, Grace said, "It's just curiosity...family history...the country I come from...it's my birth country...you know what I mean. I'm not looking for any other reason Mom. You understand, right?"

"It's okay dear, don't worry. We can find out I'm sure. Your dad and I are behind you all the way. Whatever you decide. Just don't let this overshadow your classes this semester. Okay?"

"Yes, Mom, in fact, I think this can be good for my classes."

Five years later, Greg, Josy and Grace were on a plane to Seoul again. This time for a reunion of sorts. Grace's birth mother was so happy to meet her. She was a young teenager when Grace was born and unable to support her. The father was young as well, and the parents were not going to let the two get married at that age. All the parents agreed and told the boy and girl this is what must happen. It was hard for her mom to let her go, but was assured that a wonderful family was waiting for this new baby.

Cho EunHye came up to Grace and stood there. She and her boyfriend eventually did marry and had three more children. They were all there, standing behind EunHye. Grace moved forward and put our her hand to her birth mother. EunHye took it and smiled. The translator began the conversation with introductions and from there the conversation was mostly questions and answers. When EunHye learned of Grace's name she said to Josy, through the translator, that her name meant 'grace' as well. This brought a tear and a smile to Josy's face and then she gave EunHye a hug.

Grace had brought her video camera and documented as much as EunHye would tell her. Also her three siblings talked about their mom and dad and how they grew up. Grace was finishing her masters degree in communication, and this trip was going to be the basis for her thesis project: *Finding My Families - The Process and the Meaning*. She also was going include family history from Josy and Greg, Theresa and Roger, and her grandma Sarah as well.

On the plane ride home a week later, Josy said to Grace, "I'm so glad we did this. You now have a brother and a two sisters you can write to and keep in contact with .EunHye too. And do you know what EunHye means?"

"Yes, I heard that. She and I have the same name."

"You are my grace, Grace." Josy gave her a kiss and hug.

"I am so excited to put all our family history down. I think I will love showing it to my own children someday...that is if I have any."

"All in good time...all in good time."

In good time, Bobby was born. At five he was very smart and was looking forward to his mom's book being published. Grace had told him all the stories she had learned about her family, both of them.

"Are your books here Mommy?" Bobby asked Grace as he spied the delivery box on the kitchen counter.

"I think so. Let's open the box and find out, shall we?"

Grace's first book was called 'Much More Than DNA' and documented all she learned about her family history. After all, between her grandparents on both sides and her mom, and her family in Korea, there was a lot to tell. She talked of how Bobby was born to her. As a single mom, she was thankful for her mom Josy's help when he was born. Her boyfriend didn't want to be a father and bristled at the idea of bringing another child into this "Messed up world." Grace, being true to her name, gave him the out. Their relationship was not one of love, but convenience. She really didn't understand that until the day her baby boy was born. That day, she knew what true love was.

Being a mom gave her a perspective she never had before. She cherished those first two years with just her and little Bobby. And those years prepared her for the day she met her Michael, Michael Stuart. They hit it off right away, and now she knew what a soul mate was. They had been together for three years now. Before Michael and Grace got together, she and little Bobby lived with Josy and Greg, now called Nanas and Papas. Josy and Greg loved having them there, in the old house. They were the forth generation to live there.

Josy rocked the baby boy many a time sitting at the window seat looking out on that familiar yard with the trees and flowers; summer, fall, winter and spring...at least until Grace and Michael got an apartment. But she still had gramma duties; baby sitting now and then. Precious times they were.

It was a fall day. The oranges and yellows, browns, as well as the rain, reminded Josy of her wedding day so many years ago. She remembered Greg's vows, her mom looking so proud and Greg's parents too. Mama H. was there beside her holding her flowers and so proud as well. Josy felt so warm as she realized the grace and blessings she had been shown in her life. Yes, the dark times were there, but overall she was just thankful for the life she had lived. It was lonelier now, with Greg's passing and of course Theresa and Roger's as well. Grace and her family were in California now. Grace had become a producer of documentaries on family history. She was putting many family histories in video archives. It was very rewarding work. Josy was so proud of her. She traveled quite a lot around the country filming and interviewing people. And when she was anywhere near home, she would spend as much time as she could with Josy.

Retirement wasn't hard for Josy, but selling the business was. She could not let go completely, so she kept ownership of the building...the O'l Gas Station. She was friendly with the new owners and would stop in now and then for a chat. Then she would head over to the diner and meet Mama H. for lunch. It was quite different now, under new ownership and remodeled. Franky retired too, and so it was certainly not the same as it was when she was there as a teen working for Mama H. But the name was the same, Humphries Diner, and the food was...almost as good.

It was just Josy and Mama H. now. Even though Mama H. was nearing the century mark, she still was able to drive and live alone. When they weren't meeting at the diner, Josy would have her over for tea quite often and they would spend the afternoons reminiscing and enjoying each other's company.

EunHye kept in contact with Josy as well. Over the years they had become pen pals, and they compared 'mom' stories. Though thousands of miles away, and very different cultures, the love of a mom was the same. Josy enjoyed the letters they shared.

Josy would fly out to California for the holidays and just loved visiting Grace, Michael and Robert...as he now preferred to be called. He was in high school and loved surfing, skateboarding and music. He was learning to play guitar...and of course wanted to start a band. Josy would encourage him to chase his dreams no matter where they might lead.

Returning home from her visits was always hard, for Josy, but still, there was her window seat. Like a treasure chest, it housed all the memories. All the hours she enjoyed in that special place, would never be forgotten. They were in Grace's book now, not to mention the video archive. Those memories would live on and be shared by her entire family.

Josy sat at the window seat one evening with a cup of chamomile tea just watching the winter snows and the Christmas lights when the phone rang...Josy picked it up...the voice on the line said, "Hello, is this Josephine Daudry?"

"Yes, who is this?"

"Umm, my name is....Lacey MacClean."

To be continued...

The Josephine Daudry Trilogy

Get Them All!

Enjoy the full story of Josy, Greg, and their families with all the adventures, and miss-adventures that they go through. Then find out about this fantasy woman, Lacey MacClean.

These three books are perfect for reading on a trip by plane or as a passenger by train, bus, or car. They are short reads; entertaining and easy. Take them camping or sit by the fireplace for a nice cozy evening.

Printed in the United States
by Baker & Taylor Publisher Services